MODULE

1

WORLD OF WORK

Best Practice
Pre-Intermediate

BUSINESS ENGLISH IN CONTEXT

Coursebook

THOMSON

United Kingdom • United States • Australia • Canada • Mexico • Singapore • Spain

Contents

This module looks at work around the world and at some of the things that almost everyone has to deal with: meetings, projects and working as part of a team.

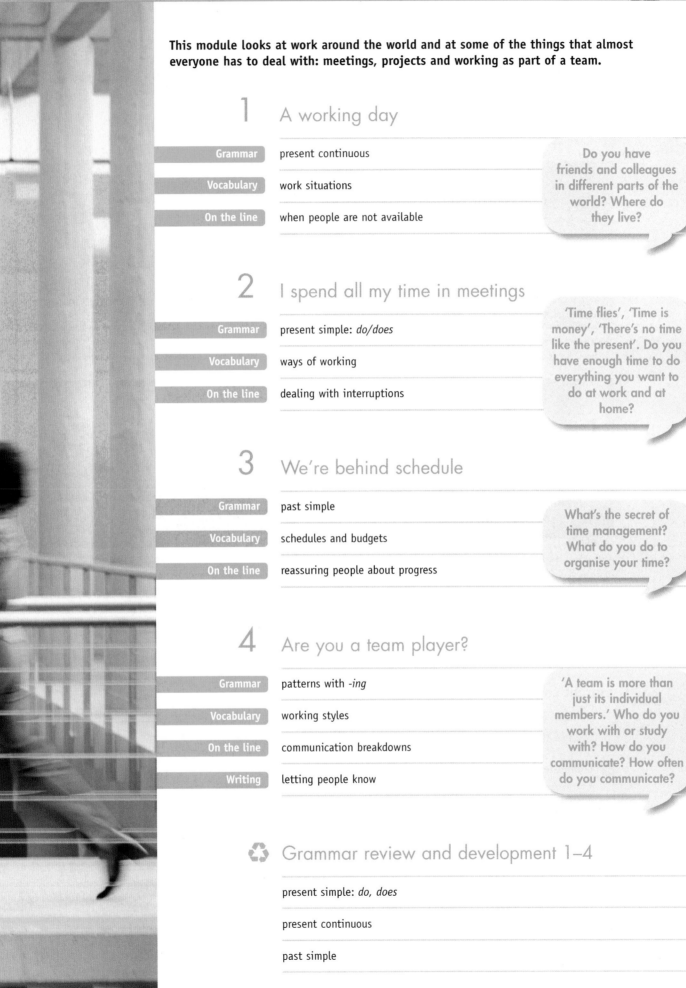

1 A working day

Grammar	present continuous
Vocabulary	work situations
On the line	when people are not available

> Do you have friends and colleagues in different parts of the world? Where do they live?

2 I spend all my time in meetings

Grammar	present simple: *do/does*
Vocabulary	ways of working
On the line	dealing with interruptions

> 'Time flies', 'Time is money', 'There's no time like the present'. Do you have enough time to do everything you want to do at work and at home?

3 We're behind schedule

Grammar	past simple
Vocabulary	schedules and budgets
On the line	reassuring people about progress

> What's the secret of time management? What do you do to organise your time?

4 Are you a team player?

Grammar	patterns with *-ing*
Vocabulary	working styles
On the line	communication breakdowns
Writing	letting people know

> 'A team is more than just its individual members.' Who do you work with or study with? How do you communicate? How often do you communicate?

♻ Grammar review and development 1–4

present simple: *do, does*

present continuous

past simple

1 A working day

Reading **A** Read about these people.

Alvaro is a coffee grower in Brazil. He's visiting the warehouse to check the quality of the coffee. This year, it's very good.

Daljit is a video games developer in Bangalore. She's in a meeting with her team. They're discussing a new project.

Monique is a buyer for a department store in Paris. She's having lunch with a colleague. They're talking about their boss.

Taro is a company boss in Kyoto. He's singing in a karaoke bar with an overseas business partner. They're having a good time!

B Work in pairs. Ask and answer questions about the four people.

A: *What's Alvaro doing?*

B: *He's visiting the warehouse*

Grammar **present continuous**

*Monique **is having** lunch with a colleague.*

You use the present continuous to talk about an activity in progress now.

A Complete the table.

What are you doing?	I'm (I am) writing an e-mail.
What's (What is) she doing?	She's (She is) having lunch with a colleague.
What are they doing?	They're (They are) driving home.

B Complete the questions and answers with the correct forms of the verbs in brackets.

1 Pilar is a company receptionist in New York.

'Where's Pilar going (go) right now?'

'She's ___ (take) the subway to work.'

2 Sonia is a tour guide in Prague.

'Who ___ Sonia ___ (talk) to right now?'

'She ___ (talk) to a group of tourists.'

3 Rachid is an oil worker in Kuwait.

'What ___ he ___ (do) right now?'

'He ___ (take) a break and ___ (drink) tea.'

4 Peng is a factory manager in China.

'What ___ he ___ (watch) on television right now?'

'He ___ (watch) an old James Bond film.'

■ More information:
Grammar review
and development
page 15
Grammar overview
page 98
▶ More practice:
Workbook page 2

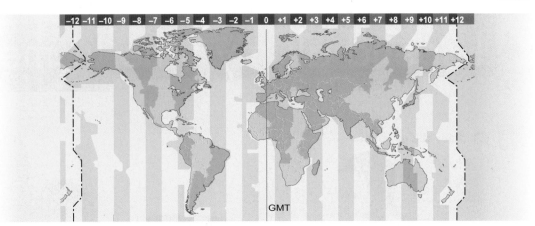

-12 -11 -10 -9 -8 -7 -6 -5 -4 -3 -2 -1 0 +1 +2 +3 +4 +5 +6 +7 +8 +9 +10 +11 +12

GMT

Speaking

A **The time is 12 noon in London. Calculate the time in these cities.**

1 Rio _8 am_ 3 Sydney _____ 5 Kyoto _____

2 New York _____ 4 Paris _____ 6 Kuwait _____

B **It is still 12 noon in London. Match the questions to the answers.**

Is it a good time to phone someone in ...

1 Los Angeles? a No, it's quite late in the evening there now. Phone them tomorrow.

2 Paris? b No, it's the middle of the night there. Wait till late this afternoon.

3 Wellington? c No, they're having lunch there. Try phoning a bit later.

C **Now practise saying the questions and answers in pairs.**

D **Work in pairs. Ask and answer about the other places in exercise A.**

A: *Is it a good time to phone someone in Kyoto?*

B: *No, it's the evening there. They're having dinner.*

Vocabulary

A **Use the expressions in the box to talk about where your colleagues are.**

*Susan isn't here today. She's **ill and off work**.*

at work	working at home	out of the office
out to lunch	~~ill and off work~~	in a meeting
on holiday	on a business trip	

ON THE LINE **A** 🔘 1.1 **Listen to the four telephone conversations. In which conversations do you hear each of these expressions?**

a I'm afraid she's in a meeting. Can you call back later? [3] e Sorry to call you so late. [ ]

b OK. I have the number. [ ] f You can call him there if you like. [ ]

c OK. I'll send her an e-mail. [ ] g That's OK. I'll call her on her mobile. [ ]

d She's out to lunch. Can I take a message? [ ] h That's all right. [ ]

Your turn

B **Work in pairs. Student A looks at this page. Student B looks at page 149.**

Student A

You want to speak to Maya Nolan at Trendex. *Can I speak to Maya Nolan, please?*

You try to phone her four times, but each time she is not available.

1 Say you'll try again later. *I'll try again later.*

2 Say you'll call her on her mobile.

3 Say you'll call her at the warehouse.

4 Say you'll phone again next week.

Checklist

✓ present continuous: He's singing in a karaoke bar.

✓ say where people are: off work, in a meeting ...

✓ contact people: I'll call her at home.

2 I spend all my time in meetings

Reading

A Study the pie chart.

This is how Daljit spends her time in a typical working week, Monday to Friday (120 hours).

Listening to music — Hobby: learning the guitar
Watching television — Reading — Meetings — Writing and answering e-mails
Playing with her children — CHOICE TIME — WORK TIME
Housework — Cooking — Shopping — Writing reports
Showering, dressing — PERSONAL TIME — Travelling to and from work
Sleeping

B Draw a similar pie chart for you.

Your turn **C** Work in pairs. Ask and answer questions about your pie charts.

A: *Do you spend a lot of time in meetings?*
B: *Yes, I do. About twenty hours a week.*

Grammar

present simple: *do/does*

***Do you** write a lot of reports?*
You use *do* and *does* to ask about general situations and routines.

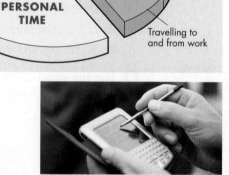

A PDA is a personal digital assistant.

A Complete the table.

_Do_ you use a PDA?	Yes, I do. / No, I don't.
Why _____ you use a PDA?	Because I can check my e-mail when I'm out of the office.
_____ Daljit use a PDA?	Yes, she does. / No, she doesn't.
Why _____ she use a PDA?	Because she prefers using her laptop and mobile phone.

Your turn **B** Work in pairs. Ask and answer questions about how you manage your time.

A: *Each morning, do you make a list of everything you have to do?*
B: *No, I don't. I know what I have to do.*

1 Each morning, make a list of everything you have to do.
2 Prioritise each task.
3 Only spend the time that is necessary on each task.
4 Tell colleagues to leave you alone when you are working on something.
5 Clear your desk at the end of each day.

■ More information:
Grammar review and development page 14
Grammar overview page 97

▶ More practice:
Workbook page 4

C Now talk about your findings like this.

... doesn't make lists. She says she has everything in her head.
... tells colleagues not to disturb him when he's working on something.

Vocabulary and listening

A 🔊 2.1 Listen to the people. Which of the expressions in the box do they use talking about themselves?

| ~~punctual~~   ~~organised~~   get on well with people |
| good with computers   tidy   nice   efficient |
| in a good mood   good with detail   polite |

1: <u>organised</u> _____ _____ _____

2: <u>punctual</u> _____ _____ _____

B 🔊 2.2 Listen to the people. Which of the expressions in the box do they use talking about colleagues?

| disorganised   late   complete mess |
| ~~hopeless with computers~~   untidy |
| inefficient   ~~in a bad mood~~   rude |

A: <u>in a bad mood</u> _____ _____ _____

B: <u>hopeless with computers</u> _____ _____ _____

ON THE LINE **A** 🔊 2.3 Listen to the three telephone conversations. In which conversations do you hear each of these expressions?

a in an interview ___   b in a meeting _1_   c preparing a presentation ___

B Listen again. What do Daljit and the caller agree to in each conversation? Write the number and the exact words.

Exact words:

a The caller offers to send an e-mail. ___ _____ .

b The caller asks if she can phone Daljit later. ___ _____ .

c Daljit offers to phone the caller later. _1_ <u>Can I call you back later?</u> _____

Your turn **C** Practise the conversations in pairs.

Student A (answers the phone)	Student B (makes the call)
Say who you are. *... speaking.*	Say hello. *Hello ... This is ...* Ask if this is a good time to call.
Say it isn't and give a reason. (Use the situations in exercise A.)	
	Suggest what to do.
Agree.	
Say goodbye.	Say goodbye.

Checklist

✓ present simple questions: *Do you use a PDA? Does he use a PDA?*

✓ ways of working: *punctual, organised, not very good with computers ...*

✓ interruptions: *'Is this a good time to call?' 'Can you call back later?*

3 We're behind schedule

Listening

A Study the stages in this project schedule for a video game.

Crazy Raiders – project schedule

Stages	Year 1							Year 2								
	J	J	A	S	O	N	D	J	F	M	A	M	J	J	A	S	O
Finalise game design	✔	✔	✔														
Recruit developers		✔	✔														
Write software																	
Design packaging																	
Manufacture product																	
Launch product																	

B **3.1** It is now May in Year 1. Listen to Daljit's presentation about the schedule. Complete the schedule with the other stages in the project.

Grammar

past simple

Did they find enough developers?
*No, they **didn't**. They needed fifty and they only found twenty.*

You use the past simple to talk something that happened in the past.

A Complete the table.

■ More information:
Grammar review
and development
page 15
Grammar overview
page 99

▶ More practice:
Workbook page 6

Regular verbs		Irregular verbs	
finalise	finalised	find	found
need	_____	go	_____
recruit	_____	write	_____

Reading and speaking

A Read the memo and underline all the verbs in the past simple.

From: Daljit Khan   **Date:** 30th June 200-
To: Keith Jones   **Subject:** Crazy Raiders schedule

For various reasons, the project is behind schedule. The game design stage <u>went</u> OK and they finalised it ahead of schedule, at the end of July last year.

Our problems started just after that. We needed to recruit fifty developers, but at first, we only found twenty – last July there were many other companies who wanted to recruit the same people. We only finished recruitment in December last year. So the software writing stage started two months late, and only finished last month.

The packaging designers started work on schedule, but we didn't like their work. We looked for another design company, and what they did was very good, but we lost a month, and the work is only ending now.

There were technical problems at the factory and manufacturing is starting three months late, in August. We can still launch the product in September, but with lower stocks of finished video games than we planned. Another problem is that we are over budget by 20 per cent!

B It is now June in Year 2. Correct the project schedule in Listening exercise A using the information in the memo.

C Complete the definitions with the expressions in the box.

| over budget | behind schedule | within budget | ~~ahead of schedule~~ | under budget | on schedule |

1 If you finish a project <u>ahead of schedule</u>, you finish it early.
2 If you finish a project _____ _____, you finish it on time.
3 If you finish a project _____ _____, you finish it late.
4 If you finish a project _____ _____, it costs less than you planned.
5 If you finish a project _____ _____, it costs exactly what you planned.
6 If you finish a project _____ _____, it costs more than you planned.

Your turn

D Work in pairs. Student A is one of Daljit's colleagues in another department. Student B is Daljit. Use the corrected schedule to ask and answer questions about what happened with the project. (Don't look at the memo!)

A: *When did you finish recruiting the developers?*   **B:** *In December.*

ON THE LINE A 3.2 Listen to the conversation between Daljit and her colleague, Keith, in London. Listen for these words and write out the complete expressions in which you hear them.

1 delays <u>I'm rather worried about the delays.</u>   4 disaster _____.
2 bother _____.   5 rush _____.
3 tight _____.   6 panic _____.

Your turn

B Student A looks at this page. Student B turns to page 149.

Student A

• You are Keith. Ask Daljit (Student B) about actual spending on the Crazy Raiders project. *We planned to spend $300,000 on designing the game. How much did we actually spend?*

• Complete the table.

Budget (US$)	Planned	Actual
Design game	300,000	450,000
Write software	750,000	
Design packaging	7,000	
Manufacture product	92,000	
TOTAL	1,149,000	

Checklist

✓ past simple: *We didn't recruit enough developers.*   ✓ schedules and budgets: *tight schedule, over budget ...*   ✓ reassure people about progress: *Don't panic!*

4 Are you a team player?

Reading and speaking

Your turn

A Work in pairs. Ask and answer questions based on the statements about you.

Do you like working on your own?

1 I like working on my own.
2 I'm good at communicating with colleagues.
3 I like being by myself for some of the day.
4 I like finishing things.
5 I'm good at getting others to work together.
6 I enjoy sharing an office/workspace with other people.
7 I like helping colleagues if they come to me with a problem.
8 I have a lot of new ideas, but after a project starts, I like others to finish it.
9 I'm a team player.

B Now talk about your partner.

... doesn't like working on her own.

Grammar **patterns with -ing**

*She likes **being** part of a team.*
*She's very good at **helping** colleagues.*

Some verbs and expressions are followed by -ing forms.

A Complete the sentences with the correct forms of the verbs in brackets.

1 He prefers working (work) with others to working on his own.
2 I hate _____ (eat) on my own in restaurants.
3 They dislike _____ (be) in the same room together.
4 I enjoy _____ (drive) to work – it gives me time to be by myself and to think.
5 We should finish _____ (test) the software before giving it to users.
6 She's terrible at _____ (keep) records of what she does.
7 He's bad at _____ (tell) other people what's happening.

■ More information: Grammar overview page 98
▶ More practice: Workbook page 8

ON THE LINE **A** 🔊 4.1 **Listen to four conversations between colleagues. What is each conversation about?**

a a meeting ___ b a report ___ c a visitor ___ d a delivery _1_

B 🔊 4.2 **Now listen to the conversations again and to how they continue. Which expression do you hear in each one – a or b?**

1 a I left a message – I guess you'd already left the office.
b I left a message – I guess you'd already gone home.

2 a This week's meeting is cancelled. But we're meeting next week as usual.
b The meeting this week isn't taking place. But it's on next week as usual.

3 a This place is driving me crazy!
b This place is sending me crazy!

4 a Just go ahead and see him – and let me know what happens.
b Just go ahead with the meeting. Let me know what you decide.

Your turn **C** **Work in pairs. Student A looks at this page. Student B turns to page 149.**

> **Student A**
>
> You are Amanda. Student A is Zak, a colleague. Today is Tuesday. Tom West was coming for a job interview on Thursday at 2 pm. Zak phones you to tell you about a change in the interview time. Ask why he did not tell you before.
> *Why didn't you tell me before?*
>
> When Zak tells you about the different times he tried to contact you, explain why you didn't get his message.
> • On Monday afternoon, the window was open and the wind blew all the papers off your desk.
> • You only look at your e-mails once a week, on Friday afternoons.
> • Your voicemail isn't working properly. People can leave messages, but you don't get them.
> • Tell Zak to phone Tom West and arrange another time. Then end the conversation.

Writing **A** **Read the e-mail that Zak sent to Amanda on Monday evening.**

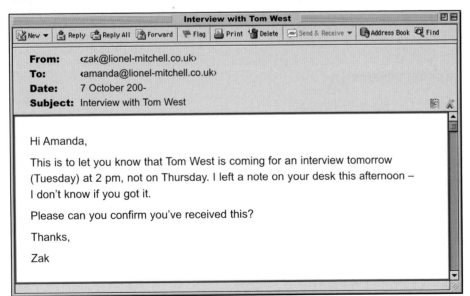

From:	‹zak@lionel-mitchell.co.uk›
To:	‹amanda@lionel-mitchell.co.uk›
Date:	7 October 200-
Subject:	Interview with Tom West

Hi Amanda,

This is to let you know that Tom West is coming for an interview tomorrow (Tuesday) at 2 pm, not on Thursday. I left a note on your desk this afternoon – I don't know if you got it.

Please can you confirm you've received this?

Thanks,

Zak

B **Think of a change of plan in your organisation or school like the one above. Write an e-mail to a friend or colleague to tell them about it.**

Checklist ✓ patterns with *-ing*: *I enjoy sharing an office.* ✓ working styles: *on my own / by myself, team player ...* ✓ office communications: *This is just to let you know that ...*

present simple: *do/does*

Affirmative	Negative	Questions
I work.	I don't work.	Do you work?
He/she works.	He/she doesn't work.	Does he/she work?

*I **spend** a lot of time on the phone.*

***Does** the company make hi-tech products?*

You use the present simple to talk about general situations and facts.

Ⓐ Complete this company description with the correct verbs in brackets.

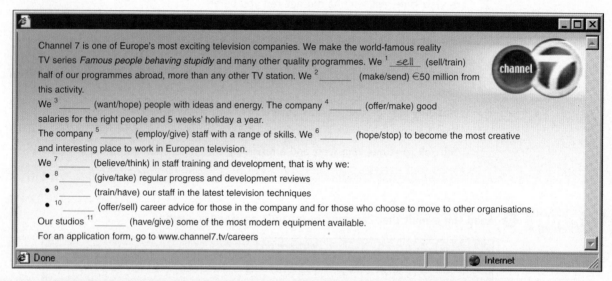

Channel 7 is one of Europe's most exciting television companies. We make the world-famous reality TV series *Famous people behaving stupidly* and many other quality programmes. We ¹ _sell_ (sell/train) half of our programmes abroad, more than any other TV station. We ² _____ (make/send) €50 million from this activity.

We ³ _____ (want/hope) people with ideas and energy. The company ⁴ _____ (offer/make) good salaries for the right people and 5 weeks' holiday a year.

The company ⁵ _____ (employ/give) staff with a range of skills. We ⁶ _____ (hope/stop) to become the most creative and interesting place to work in European television.

We ⁷ _____ (believe/think) in staff training and development, that is why we:

- ⁸ _____ (give/take) regular progress and development reviews
- ⁹ _____ (train/have) our staff in the latest television techniques
- ¹⁰ _____ (offer/sell) career advice for those in the company and for those who choose to move to other organisations.

Our studios ¹¹ _____ (have/give) some of the most modern equipment available.

For an application form, go to www.channel7.tv/careers

present simple: adverbs

*I **always** have corn flakes for breakfast.*

*She doesn't **often** go to the opera.*

You can use the present simple to talk about routines. In that case, you can use the present simple with the adverbs in the box. You usually put these adverbs in front of the verb.

always	often	usually	sometimes	never

Ⓑ You are interviewing the boss of Channel 7 in exercise A. Make questions (Q) and answers (A) using the adverbs in brackets.

1 Q: you sell your programmes abroad? (always)

    *Do you **always** sell your programmes abroad?*

    A: Some of our programmes are only suitable for the UK market. We sell them abroad. (not always)

2 Q: the company fire staff? (often)

    A: We fire people. (not often) We only recruit the most creative people and we make mistakes in our recruitment. (not often)

3 Q: you talk to programme makers about ideas for new programmes? (usually)

    A: discuss new programmes with them. (always)

4 Q: you and the programme makers argue? (sometimes)

    A: disagree about ideas for programmes. (sometimes)

5 Q: the company win prizes for its programmes? (often)

    A: Of course! We have a year without prizes. (never)

■ More information:
Grammar overview
page 97

▶ More practice:
Workbook page 10

present continuous: activity in progress

Affirmative	Negative	Questions
I'm working.	I'm not (am not) working.	Are you working?

*Monique **is having** lunch with a colleague.*

You can use the present continuous to talk about an activity in progress now.

A Giorgio, in your department, is out of the office. Complete the questions using the words in the box and the correct forms of the verb *to be*. Then match the questions to the answers.

> How   What   ~~Who~~   Where   Why

1 _Who_ _is_ Giorgio seeing? ——————— a Because it's a good place to talk.
2 ____ ____ they talking about? ——— b A new customer.
3 ____ ____ they meeting?   c They're reaching an agreement.
4 ____ ____ they meeting there?   d A big contract worth €100 million.
5 ____ ____ they doing?   e At the Ritz tea-room.

present continuous: temporary situations

*They**'re working** on the street so it's difficult to park.*

You can also use the present continuous to talk about temporary situations. In that case, you often use it with time expressions such as: *this week, currently, at the moment.*

B Sentences 1–5 are about temporary situations in an office this week. Complete the sentences with the correct forms of the verbs in brackets.

1 Anita is on a training course, so I _'m using_ (use) her office – it's better than mine.
2 There's a train strike, so everyone ____ (drive) to work – the traffic is terrible and people ____ (arrive) very late.
3 What's more, a lot of people are off sick, so we ____ (do) less work and customers ____ . (complain)
4 In addition, my computer ____ (not work), so I ____ (not send) any e-mails.
5 And, above all, the company ____ (reorganise), so everyone ____ (feel) very worried.

■ More information:
Grammar overview
page 98
▶ More practice:
Workbook page 11

past simple

Affirmative	Negative	Questions
They worked.	They didn't (did not) work.	Did they work?

*They **finished** the project late. They **didn't finish** it on time.*

You use the past simple to talk about completed actions in the past.

A Use the notes to make questions and answers about what happened with Crazy Raiders, the video game in Unit 3.

What Daljit wanted: **What actually happened:**
● to manufacture 500,000 games before the launch.   They made 250,000 games.

Q: *They wanted to manufacture 500,000 games before the launch. Did they actually manufacture 500,000?*

A: *No, they didn't. In the end, they only made 250,000.*

● to start writing Version 2 of Crazy Raiders at the end   They started at the end of the third year.
  of the first year.
● to develop the business with the partner in London.   They found a new partner in Amsterdam.
● to make a profit of $5 million in the second year.   They made a profit of $7 million.
● to write the software for two new games.   They wrote the software for four new games.

■ More information:
Grammar overview
page 98
▶ More practice:
Workbook page 11

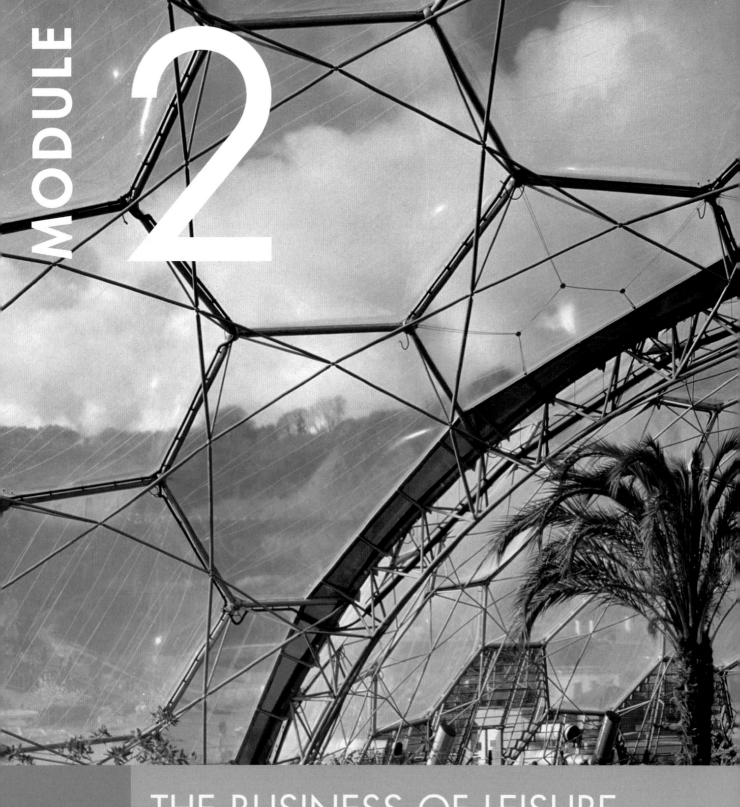

MODULE

2

THE BUSINESS OF LEISURE

Here we look at how people spend money on their homes and at some of the leisure possibilities when they go out.

5 Staying in

Listening and vocabulary

A 🔘 **5.1** **Listen to two people talking. Which speaker is the owner of which home?**

B **Listen again. Which speaker uses each of these words: 1 or 2? Which are nouns and which are adjectives?**

armchairs **1** **noun**

flowery _____ _____

screen _____ _____

thick _____ _____

clean **2** **adj**

furniture _____ _____

television _____ _____

comfortable _____ _____

heavy _____ _____

hi-tech _____ _____

traditional _____ _____

cosy _____ _____

minimalist _____ _____

typical _____ _____

ugly _____ _____

elegant _____ _____

equipment _____ _____

modern _____ _____

wooden _____ _____

C **Work in pairs. Ask and answer which room you prefer and give your reasons.**

A: *Which room do you prefer?*

B: *I like the one on the right, because it's so hi-tech.*

D **Now talk about your findings.**

... likes the one on the right because ...

Grammar

count and uncount nouns

*The sales **assistants** are so helpful.*
*Electrical **equipment** is so ugly.*

A **Complete the rules.**

*She likes comfortable **armchairs**.*
Some nouns can have a plural form. They are count nouns.

*He doesn't have a lot of **furniture**.*
Other nouns do not have a _____ form. You cannot use them with *a/an*. They are _____ .

*I'm here on **business**. / Most new **businesses** fail within five years.*
Some nouns can be both _____ and _____ .

B The nouns in the box are only uncount. Use some of them to complete the sentences.

| advice | employment | equipment | furniture | homework |
| information | knowledge | ~~money~~ | progress | traffic |

1 Some say that the purpose of business is to make money; others say that it must have social aims.

2 If you're late for a business meeting, just say that you were stuck in the _____ .

3 Those who really need _____ usually don't like it and, anyway, they are not able to follow it.

4 In this company, we have too many facts and too much _____ . But we don't know how to use it all so that it becomes real _____ .

5 Electrical _____ always breaks down when you need it most. I hate computers!

6 Levels of _____ are so high that we can't find the people we're looking for.

■ More information:
Grammar review
and development
page 105
Grammar overview
page 26

▶ More practice:
Workbook page 13

(C)N THE LINE A 🔊 **5.2** **Martin wants to order some furniture. Listen to the beginning of the conversation and underline the expressions that you hear.**

Avgard 3 piece suite — Great Value — New seasonal design

Emma

1 a This is the order department.
 b <u>You're through to the order department.</u>

2 a Emma here. What can I do for you?
 b My name's Emma. How can I help?

Martin

1 a I have your catalogue here.
 b I have your catalogue in front of me.

2 a I'd like to order some Avgard furniture.
 b I want to place an order for some furniture in the Avgard range.

B **Listen to the rest of the conversation. In which order do you hear these words?**

stock __   system __   available ⌐1⌐   guaranteed __   deliver __

C 🔊 **5.3** **It is one week later. Listen to the beginning of this conversation. Underline the expressions that you hear.**

Emma

1 a <u>Order department. Emma speaking.</u>
 b You're through to the order department. Emma here.

2 a What can I do for you?
 b How can I help?

Martin

1 a Hi! I bought some Avgard furniture from you last week.
 b Hello. I ordered some Avgard furniture from you last week.

2 a Did I speak to you?
 b Was it you I spoke to?

D **Listen to the rest of the conversation. In which order do you hear these expressions?**

exchange __   defect __   refund ⌐1⌐   credit note __

Your **turn** **E** **Work in pairs. Student A takes orders at another furniture company. This company has a different policy on refunds, returns and exchanges from Avgard. Student B is a customer who phones to ask for a refund for something that they have bought. Use some of the expressions in exercises A–D above to begin the conversation and then continue it.**

A: *You're through to the order department. ... here. What can I do for you?*

B: *I ordered some furniture from you ...*

Checklist

✓ count nouns:	✓ uncount nouns:	✓ design and style:	✓ orders and refunds:	We can't give
DVD players,	furniture,	cosy, traditional,	I'd like to order	you a refund, but
armchairs ...	equipment ...	elegant, hi-tech ...	some Avgard	we can give you
			furniture.	a credit note.

6 Museums and exhibitions

A Read this article.

Museum marketing

The Guggenheim is changing the rules about how to market a museum. And traditional museums in America and Europe don't like the change.

MUSEUMS have never had it so good. New ones are being built all over the place, and existing ones are getting bigger; money-raising campaigns have never been so successful, and visitor numbers have never been higher: American museums now attract more than a billion visitors a year.

As they have become more marketable, some museums have begun to behave in more commercial ways. And it's working. Tate Modern in London and the Guggenheim Museum in New York, two of the most commercial big museums, are doing particularly well.

This has forced the directors of all museums to ask: How far can the commercialisation of an art museum go? Which marketing techniques are acceptable, and which are not? Will there in future be two kinds of museums: the temples of high culture, and the more popular entertainment centres?

The controversy is over the marketing methods of the Guggenheim Museum. Its methods are aggressive, even by New York standards. Three years ago, the museum put on an exhibition of motorcycles sponsored by BMW, a German car maker. But it was an exhibition, last autumn, of dresses by Giorgio Armani, an Italian fashion designer, that really annoyed people. The exhibition was sponsored by *In Style*, a fashion magazine, but Mr Armani has given $15m to the museum. Some critics have called this 'rent'.

'When merchants enter the temple' *adapted from The Economist, 19 Apr 2001*

B Look at how the adjectives 1–7 are used in the article. Match them to their definitions in the middle column. Then match the adjectives to the nouns.

1 traditional	able to be sold	**a** people
2 successful	related to business	**b** tradition
3 marketable	done in a way that it has always been done	**c** success
4 commercial	good enough for a particular purpose	**d** acceptability
5 acceptable	having the wanted result	**e** commerce
6 popular	using strong methods that some people do not like	**f** aggression
7 aggressive	liked by a lot of people	**g** market

Grammar present perfect and past simple

Ⓐ **Look at the examples and complete the rules.**

*Museums **have become** more marketable.*

***Have** you **been** to a museum in the past year?*

You use the present perfect to talk about the __past__ without mentioning a specific _____ .

*Yes, I **went** to see Anish Kapoor at Tate Modern in July.*

You use the past _____ when you mention a _____ _____ .

Ⓑ **Look at the article about the Guggenheim Museum again. Underline all the verbs in the present perfect, and then double-underline all those in the past simple.**

> Your turn

Ⓒ **Work in pairs. Ask and answer about the following.**

- a film at the cinema   *Have you been to a film at the cinema recently?*
  what/who they saw   *What did you see?*

  How much they paid for the ticket; if they had a good time ...

- an opera   • a play at the theatre
- a rock concert   • a museum
- a ballet   • a classical music concert

■ More information:
Grammar overview
pages 98 and 100
Grammar review
and development
page 27

▶ More practice:
Workbook page 15

Ⓓ **Check with the whole class how many people have done these things.**

Three of us have been to a rock concert in the past year.

ⒸN THE LINE **Ⓐ** 6.1 **Listen to someone making a booking for the *Speed* exhibition at the Modern Art Museum and complete the information.**

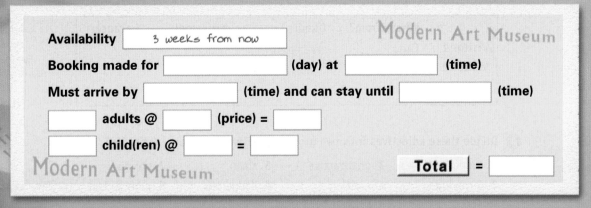

Modern Art Museum

Availability	3 weeks from now

Booking made for [ ] (day) at [ ] (time)

Must arrive by [ ] (time) and can stay until [ ] (time)

[ ] adults @ [ ] (price) = [ ]

[ ] child(ren) @ [ ] = [ ]

Total [ ] = [ ]

Modern Art Museum

Ⓑ **Now practise the call using the information from exercise A.**

A: *Autoticket. Can I help you?*

B: *Yes, I'd like some tickets for the Speed exhibition.*

Continue the call and sort out the price calculation.

B: *It's not 46 dollars, it's ...*

A: *You're right. Sorry about that.*

Checklist

✓ describing museums as entertainment: *aggressive / aggression, commercial / commerce ...*

✓ past simple compared with present perfect: *Have you been to a rock concert recently? – Yes, I saw the Stones in Singapore last month.*

✓ make a booking: *I'd like to book three tickets for Thursday.*

7 Family entertainment

Reading and listening

A Read this advertisement.

UTAH
FARWEST

COME TO FARWEST, UTAH
See how the West was won!
Watch the rodeo: see our cowboys ride wild horses.
Listen to cowboy country music: there's a show every hour. Watch cowboys cooking cowboy food. Ride on the roller coaster. Eat at one of our three restaurants: Big Steak, Gusano Loco (Mexican) or Delhi (Indian). Have a great day out at Farwest, or stay at our Farwest Ranch Hotel for a longer break.

B 7.1 Now listen to the three interviews with visitors to Farwest and complete the details.

	Where from?	liked:	criticised:	because:
Visitor 1	Paris	the rodeo		
Visitor 2				
Visitor 3				

(!) There are more than 500 theme parks in the US. Annually, they have 350 million visitors and total sales of $12 billion. Sales are growing at 5 to 10 per cent per year.

Vocabulary and speaking

A Divide these adjectives into two groups: positive (+) and negative (−).

1 comfortable +   3 unattractive −   5 clean __   7 boring __
2 terrifying __   4 exciting __   6 dangerous __   8 professional __

B Work in pairs. Student A looks at this page. Student B turns to page 150.

Student A

You are the interviewer in Reading and listening exercise B. You work in the PR department at Farwest. Student B is Mary-Jane Lomax, the director of Farwest.

- When Mary-Jane asks, tell her the main points from the three interviews. Use the table in Reading and listening exercise B. *The first visitor I spoke to was a woman from Paris, on vacation with her family.*

- Ask Mary-Jane for the average satisfaction score for each of the different attractions at the theme park: rodeo, country music, cowboy cooking, roller coaster, restaurants, Ranch Hotel. Take notes. *What's the average satisfaction score for the rodeo?*

- Ask Mary-Jane for the overall satisfaction score for all six attractions. *What's the overall satisfaction score for all the attractions?*

- Ask Mary-Jane for typical comments for the different attractions at *Farwest*. Take notes. *What do people think of the rodeo?*

ON THE LINE **(A)** *7.2* Farwest is one of five theme parks worldwide owned by TS Leisure, a company with its headquarters in Kyoto, Japan.

Mary-Jane Lomax, Farwest's director, gets a call from Taro Suzuki, chief executive officer of TS Leisure in Kyoto. Listen and complete the information for Farwest and the other theme parks.

		Satisfaction score	No. of visitors last year
	Farwest, Utah	7.28	500,000
	Shark Paradise, Miami		
	Mountain Village, Japan		
	Future City, France		
	Kings and Queens, UK		

(B) Listen again. Which of these expressions do you hear? In what order?

Just a moment, __   Maybe. __   Yes, but ... __

Before you go on, ... _1_   I wouldn't say that. __   Let me just finish ... __

(C) Student A is Taro Suzuki. Student B is Sandrine Simoneau, director of Future City in France. Future City also has disappointing figures. Have a similar phone call to the one between Taro and Mary-Jane. Taro ends by inviting Sandrine to Kyoto for a discussion.

Roleplay **(A)** Taro Suzuki, boss of TS Leisure, asks all his theme park directors to come to Kyoto to discuss future investment in the parks.

Student A looks at this page. Other students turn to page 151.

Student A

You are Taro Suzuki. You have a budget of $4,000,000. Ask each of your directors in turn:

* to explain the investment they want to make in their park and how much it will cost.
  How much will this investment cost?

* how many more visitors there will be and how much the satisfaction score will improve. Encourage each director to say why their investment will be better than the others.
  Why do you think your investment will be more profitable than the others?

* When you have listened to all the arguments, decide which projects you are going to invest in. (For Shark Paradise, you can reduce the number of new sharks that you buy!)

Writing **(A)** You are Taro Suzuki. Write a memo to your theme park directors explaining your decision and giving your reasons. Begin like this:

MEMO

From: Taro Suzuki   Date: 2 June 200-
To: all TS Leisure theme park directors   Subject: Future investment

Thank you for coming to Kyoto last week for a very useful meeting. I hope you all had a pleasant trip back home.
I have thought long and hard about investment in the group's theme parks.
I have decided to ... because ...

Checklist ✓ opinion adjectives: ✓ interrupt: ✓ disagree: ✓ explain a decision:
   exciting, boring,   *Before you go on ...*   *I wouldn't say that.*   *I have decided to ...*
   unattractive ...   *because ...*

8 Leisure in 2050

Reading and speaking

A Read these predictions for leisure 50 years from now.

People will spend less time at work. The average working week will be 30 hours, but most people will work from home, most of the time. Colleagues will meet once a week or once a month. Companies' headquarters buildings will still exist, with very impressive architecture, but almost no one will actually work in them. Most employees will get at least 10 weeks' holiday per year.

All forms of 'extreme' physical activity will be very popular – everything from mountaineering to bungee-jumping. National Parks, especially, will be very crowded. In summer, there will be people waiting in line to reach the tops of mountains such as Mont Blanc. There will be a charge for entry to National Parks. On the most popular days the charge will be higher in order to limit numbers.

Football will still be the world's biggest sport, and Real Madrid will still be the richest club, with the second and third richest clubs in Asia. International ownership will be normal – most big European clubs will have Asian or American owners. Football (soccer) will become the national sport of the US – baseball and American football will be much less popular than they are today.

Your turn > **B** Work in groups of three. Discuss the predictions, make some of your own and discuss them with the rest of the class.

Grammar *will* and *may, might, could* for predictions

A Look at the table and then complete the rules.

	will		
Football	might	(not)	still be the most popular sport.
	may		
	could	—	

You use *will* to say that something in the <u>future</u> is quite certain.

You use *might, may* or *could* to say that it is _____, but not certain, that something will happen in the future.

B Change these predictions for 2050 to show that they are not certain.

1 China will be the world's biggest economy.

In 2050, China might be the world's biggest economy.

2 London, Paris and New York will still be the most important world cities for business and the arts.

3 English will still be the main language of international communication.

4 Roads will be less crowded – there will be much less commuting. Cars will just be for leisure use in the country and between cities.

5 Climate change, with increased temperatures, means that skiing will no longer be possible in Europe in resorts below 3000 metres.

6 Climate change also means that northern Europe will have a more Mediterranean-type climate. Countries like Sweden and Denmark will produce wine!

■ More information:
Grammar review
and development
page 27
Grammar overview
page 101

▶ More practice:
Workbook page 19

Vocabulary **A** Complete the text using the words and expressions in the box.

| crystal ball | forecasts | ~~futurology~~ | objectives | predictions | strategy | trends |

'Hi, I'm Miranda Rees. I'm a futurologist at Crystal Ball Consultants. Of course, ¹*futurology* is not an exact science, and some say it's like looking into a ² _____ . That's the reason for our name — it's a sort of joke.

Some ³ _____ for the next fifty years are already becoming clear. We can make ⁴ _____ or ⁵ _____ based on those trends.

A ⁶ _____ is a plan or series of plans for achieving success. The plans usually involve finance, people and assets — equipment, buildings, know-how, etc. How are they going to be used to reach particular ⁷ _____ ? A company's senior executives must decide on a strategy and to do this they need to take a long-term view based on long-term trends.'

ON THE LINE **A** 🔊 8.1 Miranda Rees phones Taro Suzuki, CEO of TS Leisure, the Japanese multinational. Listen to the way Miranda shows interest in what Taro is saying. In which order do you hear her say these expressions? (She says some of them twice.)

| OK. _1_ | Right. ___ | Aha ... ___ |
| Yes ... ___ | And what about ... ___ | Really! ___ |

B Listen again and complete the table.

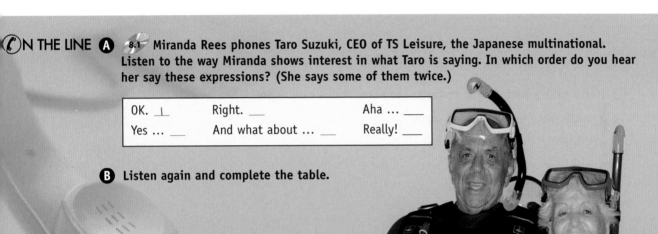

TS leisure	Now	In 10 years
Theme parks	6	9
TS Leisure Clubs		
TS Leisure Senior Clubs		
Films with actors		
Animated films		

Your turn **C** Work in pairs. Student A is Miranda. Student B is Taro.

Student A
Ask about Taro's plans for the future.
What are your plans for the next 10 years?
Show interest using the expressions in exercise A.

Student B
Use the figures above to talk about TS Leisure's plans for the next 10 years. This time you are less certain about them. Use *might, may* and *could*
We may make more animated films.

Checklist ✓ *will* and *might, may, could*:
China might become the world's biggest economy.
✓ nouns for talking about the future:
trend, forecast, prediction ...
✓ show interest:
Really!

count and uncount nouns

*You can buy DVD **players** at Wal-Mart for $19.*

Some nouns are count nouns. They can have a plural form.

*It's not going to be easy - we don't have the right **equipment**.*

Other nouns are uncount. You cannot use them with *a/an*. They do not have a plural form.

*He told us about his **experiences** in South America.*
*She has 20 years' **experience** as an accountant at ICI.*

Some nouns can be both count and uncount.

***a piece of** furniture*   ***an item of** information*

You can sometimes refer to one example of an uncount noun by using *item* or *piece* in front of it.

***information** facts*   ***insurance** policies*

And you can use count nouns to refer to particular examples of uncount nouns.

Ⓐ Match each uncount noun to the count noun that it relates to.

1 employment	**a** euros
2 travel	**b** cars
3 equipment	**c** jobs
4 traffic	**d** games
5 trouble	**e** machines
6 fun	**f** problems
7 money	**g** journeys

count and uncount nouns: activities

*I do a lot of **cooking**.*

-ing nouns are also uncount nouns.

*Do you do **a lot of** cooking?*
*Do you do **much** cooking?*

You can ask questions about uncount nouns for activities using *a lot of* or *much*.

You can answer:

*Yes, I do **a lot of** cooking.*
*No, I don't do **a lot of** cooking. / No, I don't do **much** cooking.*

Ⓑ Work in pairs. Ask and answer questions about these activities.

A	B
1 Do you do a lot of reading?	<u>No, I don't do much reading</u>. I only read about one book a year – when I'm on holiday.
2 ... shopping?	_____ . I hate shops – I go shopping as little as possible.
3 ... cooking?	_____ . I have three children and we never eat out.
4 ... entertaining?	_____ . We invite friends round at least twice a month.
5 ... gardening?	_____ . I only have a window box!

■ More information:
Grammar overview
page 105

▶ More practice:
Workbook page 21

 Ⓒ Work in pairs. Ask and answer the same questions about yourselves.

present perfect and past simple

*I **haven't been** to the cinema recently.*
*I **went** to the cinema yesterday.*
You use the present perfect to talk about the past when you don't mention a specific time.
You use the simple past when you mention a specific time.

A It is 2050. Mayumi Suzuki, Taro Suzuki's grand-daughter, is now in charge of TS Leisure (Unit 7). She gives an interview about the company's development. Complete the text with the correct forms of the verbs in brackets. Be careful with the question forms.

> **Q** When ¹ _did_ your grandfather _start_ (start) the company?
>
> **MS** He ² _____ (start) TS Leisure in 1989 when he ³ _____ (be) 30.
>
> **Q** How fast ⁴ _____ it _____ (grow)?
>
> **MS** At first, it ⁵ _____ (grow) very fast. He ⁶ _____ (open) a lot of theme parks and he ⁷ _____ (develop) our film activities. But he ⁸ _____ (stop) using real actors in 2020 because they ⁹ _____ (be) difficult to work with. Growth ¹⁰ _____ (be) fastest in the years 2020 to 2040.
>
> **Q** ¹¹ _____ the last 10 years _____ (be) so good?
>
> **MS** No, they ¹² _____ not _____ (be) so good. Growth rates in the whole leisure industry ¹³ _____ (fell), and we ¹⁴ _____ (make) lower profits. In 2042, we ¹⁵ _____ (buy) another leisure company, Country Parks. Over the past eight years, we ¹⁶ _____ (try) to improve results there, but we ¹⁷ _____ not _____ (succeed).

- More information: Grammar overview pages 98 and 100
- More practice: Workbook page 20

will and *may, might, could* for predictions

	will might may	(not)	
Football			still be the most popular sport.
	could	—	

You use *will* to say that something will quite certainly happen in the future.
You use *might, may* or *could* to say that it is possible, but not certain, that something will happen in the future.

A The mayor of Megalopolis is talking about the effects of a new tax (€10 a day) on people driving into the city centre. Where does each extract (a–e) go?

We want to limit the number of people driving into Megalopolis by charging drivers €10 a day to do so. Like all plans, it may or may not have the effects that we want.

And ¹ _b_. But the main aim is to reduce traffic. We ² ___. We are increasing the number of buses on the roads, ³ ___. Shop owners are complaining – ⁴ ___, but ⁵ ___.

a because we think that the number of passengers could rise by 35 per cent

b it will certainly have effects that we have not thought of

c might reduce the number of people driving into the centre by 20 per cent

d they say that the number of shoppers will fall

e we think that the number may actually rise with better public transport

- More information: Grammar overview page 101
- More practice: Workbook page 21

MODULE

3

DON'T OVERDO IT!

This module deals with employee fitness, considers the pressures that many people at work are under, and looks at the balance between life at work and outside.

9 Getting fit

Grammar	comparatives and superlatives
Vocabulary	describing facilities
On the line	prices and discounts

> Are you fit? What's the secret of keeping fit? Should businesses get involved in the fitness of their employees?

10 Asleep on the job?

Vocabulary	how people feel
On the line	a research interview
Writing	a report about working habits

> Are you a day person or a night person? When do you feel most tired during the day? What do you do to try to prevent this?

11 Dealing with stress

Grammar	*must* and *should*
Vocabulary	health and stress
On the line	phoning to say you can't come to work

> What are the most stressful situations at work or where you study? What do you do to reduce stress? Are people under more stress than 30 years ago? Why / why not?

12 Work-life balance

Grammar	present perfect with *for* and *since*
Vocabulary	job applications
On the line	an invitation to an interview
Writing	an e-mail job application

> How important should work or study be? What can you do to make sure that it doesn't become too important? What's the best way to keep a good balance between your work/study and your personal life?

Grammar review and development 9–12

comparatives and superlatives

must and *should*

present perfect with *for* and *since*

9 Getting fit

A Read the article.

Home from home

'Smell that?' asks Brocas Burrows as he takes me around three floors of gymnasium at the Third Space health club near Piccadilly Circus. 'Now you mention it, yes. Very nice.' 'Exactly,' says Brocas, the club's manager. 'That's the kind of thing people pay to come here for. Everywhere you go in the Third Space, it smells good.'

It's the little things that make people pay more for the Third Space, one of London's more expensive private health clubs. 'Everything has to be perfect,' says Brocas. 'That's why there are warm, clean towels everywhere and the changing rooms are spotless. The whole place is warm and comfortable.' At the Third Space, the joining fee is £275, and the annual fee is £990 (or £99 monthly). 'The philosophy is that you have three spaces in your life – home, work and here,' says Brocas. 'It's the third most important space in our members' lives – and for some of them it's even more important.' The third space in people's lives was the church, or the pub. Now, at least for many, it's the health club. The Third Space is not so much a gym as a place that you could spend all your waking hours. 'Some of our members seem never to be anywhere but here. They work out, send some e-mails, read the papers and have something to eat – for a lot of people it's more convenient than cooking at home. It's a great place to be.'

The Tyranny of the Gym *adapted from The Guardian, 5 Jan 2004 (Stuart Jeffries)*

B Now write *T* (true) or *F* (false).

1 The Third Space health club smells nice. T
2 The club is cheap but clean. __
3 The joining fee is £250 and the annual fee is £1000. __

4 The Third Space is just a gym. __
5 For some members, the Third Space is more important than work or home. __
6 Some of the members seem to have a lot of free time. __

ON THE LINE

A 9.1 Jennifer Powell works for the Global Credit Bank in Singapore. She phones three health clubs to get quotes for health club membership for its employees. Listen to the three conversations and complete the information.

	Dynamo	Elan	Fun
Normal joining fee	S$800		
Normal annual fee			
Corporate discount offered			
Minimum number of memberships to obtain discount			40
Other facilities		café, supermarket, doctor	

B Listen again. In which conversation do you hear each of these expressions?

a What are your facilities like? __
b What sort of discount can you give for our employees? 1
c Let me think about the figures you gave me and I'll get back to you. __
d We have a lot of corporate clients and we offer some very good deals. __
e Please get back to me if you require further information. __
f We offer corporate discounts on our normal fees. __

Speaking **A** Student A looks at this page. Student B turns to page 151.

> **Student A**
> You are Jennifer Powell's colleague. Jennifer (Student B) has visited the three health clubs in On the line. Ask her about each health club and note down her answers.
> *How convenient is the club?*
> *How clean are the changing rooms?*
> *What's the gym like?*
> *Are there any other facilities? What are they like?*

B Now talk about the three health clubs.

Dynamo is very convenient – it's next door to the bank.

Grammar **comparatives and superlatives**

*Your gym is **cheaper** than the others.*
*Dynamo has **the best** facilities.*

A Complete the table.

	base form	comparative	superlative
one syllable	fit low	Add ____ : fitter ____	add –est: ____ lowest
____ **or more syllables**	expensive convenient	use '____': more expensive ____ ____	use 'most': ____ ____ ____ ____
irregular	good bad	better w____	b____ worst

B Talk about the three health clubs in On the line and Speaking, using comparatives and superlatives.

Elan is cheaper to join than Dynamo, but the annual fee is more expensive.

comparatives with *even*

*The equipment at Dynamo is modern, but at Elan it's **even more** modern.*

C Make sentences using *even* with the comparatives of the adjectives to talk about two golf clubs, the Algarve and the Bellevue.

1 fees – expensive
The fees at the Algarve are expensive, but the fees at the Bellevue are even more expensive.

2 facilities – good

3 course – difficult

4 waiting list – long

5 members – rich

6 clubhouse – beautiful

7 food in the restaurant – delicious

■ More information:
Grammar review and development page 38
Grammar overview page 107
▶ More practice:
Workbook page 23

Checklist
✓ comparatives and superlatives:
Fun Health Club is the cheapest.
Dynamo is the most convenient.
The equipment is even more modern.

✓ adjectives for describing facilities: *clean, convenient ...*

✓ prices and discounts:
We offer corporate discounts on our normal fees.

10 Asleep on the job?

Reading **A** Read about these three people.

> I live in the country. I get up at 5 and start work immediately. I feel great in the morning: I'm full of energy and I try to write two or three pages by lunchtime.
> I have a good lunch and in the afternoon I feel very sleepy, so I have a nap for an hour or two. I never work in the evening – I just read or listen to music.
>
> *Christine, novelist*

> I live In Singapore and I work at a bank. I just have coffee for breakfast. When I get to work, I feel quite tired and stressed, so I drink more coffee. At lunchtime I go to a health club near the office and have a sandwich or a salad at the café there. After my trip to the health club, I feel fine. I phone my colleagues in Europe – my English is much better in the afternoon!
>
> *Tommy, bank employee*

> I work in a TV studio. When I'm working on the night shift, I get up in the afternoon. I have a big 'breakfast' in the studio cafeteria and then at midnight I start work. I love working at night! I'm a night person. Around 8 in the morning, I feel exhausted and very sleepy. I go home, go to bed and sleep till 6 in the evening.
>
> *Reina, studio manager*

B Now answer the questions.

1 What does Christine do?
2 When does she work?
3 How does Tommy feel in the morning?
4 And in the afternoon?
5 Does Reina always work on the night shift?
6 How does she feel in the morning?

C Look at this graph of Christine's energy levels at different times of day. Draw a line in the graph on the right to show how you feel at different times of day.

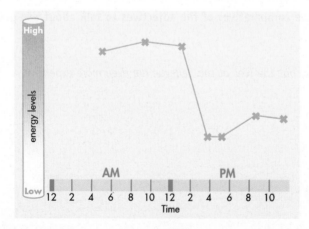

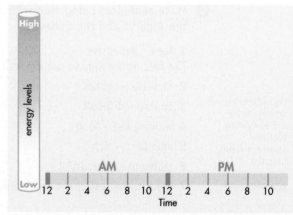

Your turn **D** Work in pairs. Explain your graph to your partner.

In the mornings I feel very sleepy, but after lunch I feel great.

> ! On average, Americans sleep 20 per cent less than they did 100 years ago – more people work in the evening, at weekends and on night shifts.

ON THE LINE **A** 10.1 A company called AR Surveys is doing research into tiredness at work. A researcher calls Tommy Chan at the bank where he works. Listen to the conversation and complete the questions.

- HOW MANY HOURS __a__ WEEK DO YOU WORK? __37__
- DO YOU _____ SHIFT WORK? _____
- WHEN DO YOU _____ AT YOUR _____ DURING THE DAY? _____
- WHEN DO YOU FEEL AT YOUR _____ ? _____
- HOW _____ DO YOU _____ FOR LUNCH? _____
- WHAT _____ YOU _____ FOR LUNCH? _____
- DO YOU _____ WINE OR BEER WITH LUNCH? _____
- HOW _____ TEA AND COFFEE DO YOU DRINK DURING THE DAY? _____

B Listen again and complete Tommy's answers.

Your turn **C** Work in pairs. Ask and answer the questions in the survey.

Speaking **A** Work in pairs. Student A looks at this page. Student B looks at page 152.

Student A

Look at the results of the research into tiredness at work. When Student B asks for it, give them the information below.

Hours	30 or less: 15%	31–40: 58%	41 or more: 27%
Shift work	Yes: 8%	No: 92%	—
People feel at their best	morning: 36%	afternoon: 34%	evening: 30%
People feel at their worst	morning: 33%	afternoon: 45%	evening: 22%

Now ask Student B questions to complete the table.

How long do people take for lunch?

Time for lunch	*45 mins or less: 34%*	*45–75 mins: 57%*	*75 mins or more: 8%*	—
Type of lunch	_____	_____	_____	_____
Wine or beer with lunch	_____	_____	—	—
Tea and coffee	_____	_____	_____	_____

Writing **A** You are the research director of AR Surveys. Write a report about some of the findings in the survey above.

REPORT

AR SURVEYS

Subject: Tiredness at work

This report presents the findings of our recent research into tiredness at work.

We found that most people (58%) work between 31 and 40 hours a week. ...

Checklist ✓how people feel: *tired, sleepy, exhausted ... I feel at my best after breakfast.* ✓ask about working habits: *How many hours a week do you work?* ✓report expressions: *This report presents ... We found that ...*

33

11 Dealing with stress

Reading and listening

A Read this article by Jennifer Powell, the human resources director at the Global Credit Bank in Singapore. What do you think should go in the gaps?

Good and bad stress

People usually think that stress is a bad thing. But we all need stress in order to live interesting lives. We need 'positive stress' to get out of bed in the morning, to work well, to give good presentations and so on.

But too much stress can cause feelings of anxiety, anger and fear. The cause could be something negative like the death of a partner or losing your job. But it could even be something positive like a new partner or going on holiday. Whatever the cause, stress can lead to health problems like headaches, high blood pressure, even heart disease.

Some people deal with stress in very unhealthy ways. For example, to deal with stress you shouldn't:

1 rely on caffeine or aspirin

2 _____

3 _____

In our company we take the health of our employees very seriously. We provide ways for them to deal with stress. For example, we offer:

4 _____

5 _____

6 _____

These are just some of the ways we try to help people deal with stress.

B 🔘 **11.1** Listen to an extract from a radio interview with Jennifer, where she talks about the same things. Complete the gaps in the article with what she says.

 C Work in pairs. Ask questions about relaxing and avoiding stress.

What do you do to relax and avoid stress?

 D Now talk about your findings.

To relax, ... plays tennis twice a week.

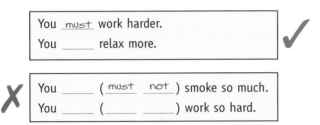

Grammar *must* and *should*

*You **must** relax more.*

*You **shouldn't** rely on aspirin to feel better.*

You use *must* and *should* to tell people what to do. *Must* is stronger than *should*.

You use *mustn't* (must not) and *shouldn't* (should not) to tell people what not to do.
Mustn't is stronger than *shouldn't*.

Ⓐ **Complete the tables.**

You <u>must</u> work harder.
You _____ relax more. ✓

✗ You _____ (<u>must</u> <u>not</u>) smoke so much.
You _____ (_____ _____) work so hard.

Ⓑ **Change the sentences about people in another company using the negative form of *should* or *must* and the words in brackets.**

1 They should smoke less. (smoke / so much) <u>They shouldn't smoke so much.</u>
2 They must get more exercise. (be / so lazy)
3 They should take more time off. (work / so hard)
4 They should drink more water. (drink / so much coffee)
5 They must go to evening classes. (watch / so much television)
6 They must eat better. (eat / so many hamburgers)

■ More information:
Grammar review
and development
page 38
Grammar overview
page 102

 Ⓒ **Give yourself some advice! Tell the class about it.**

I should get more exercise.

ⓄN THE LINE **Ⓐ** 🔊 *11.2* **Tommy Chan phones the human resources department at Global Credit Bank.**
Listen and write *T* (true) or *F* (false).

1 Tommy phones to say he can't come to work today. T
2 He's taking three days off work. ___
3 He's off work because he has a head injury. ___
4 He's seeing a doctor next week. He'll know then if
he will be able to come back to work. ___
5 He'll definitely be back at work next week. ___

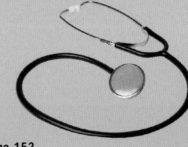

 Ⓑ **Work in pairs. Student A looks at this page. Student B looks at page 152.**

Student A

It is one month later. You work in the Human Resources department of Global Credit Bank.
Tommy Chan (Student B) phones you again to say that he can't come to work.
Start like this: *Hello. Human Resources. How can I help?*

• Ask Tommy how long he will be off work, and finish the conversation.
• Then have two more similar conversations with Tommy. (Tommy is off work quite often!)

Checklist
✓ *must, should, mustn't,*
shouldn't: You shouldn't
smoke so much.

✓ adjectives and nouns to
describe health: *ill / illness,*
healthy / health ...

✓ explain why you can't come to work:
I can't come to work today because ...
I need to take a week off work.

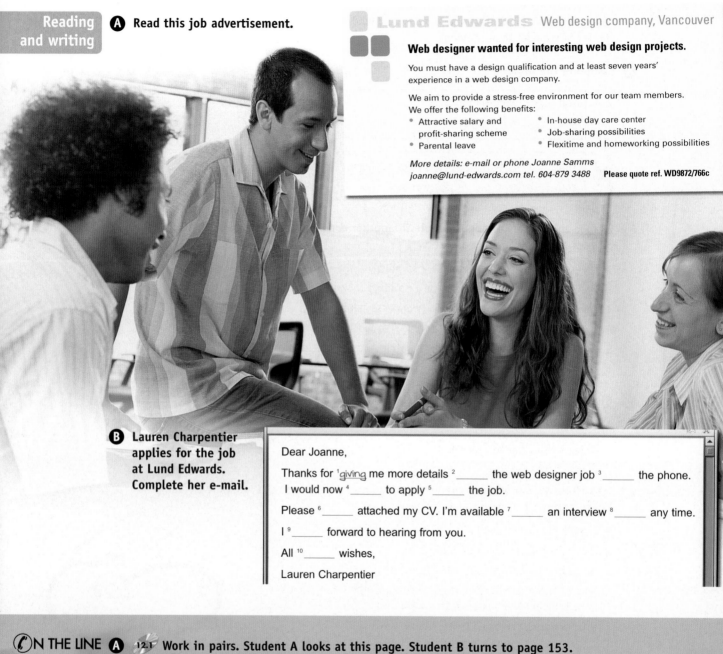

Reading and writing

A Read this job advertisement.

Lund Edwards Web design company, Vancouver

Web designer wanted for interesting web design projects.

You must have a design qualification and at least seven years' experience in a web design company.

We aim to provide a stress-free environment for our team members. We offer the following benefits:

- Attractive salary and profit-sharing scheme
- Parental leave
- In-house day care center
- Job-sharing possibilities
- Flexitime and homeworking possibilities

More details: e-mail or phone Joanne Samms
joanne@lund-edwards.com tel. 604-879 3488   Please quote ref. WD9872/766c

B Lauren Charpentier applies for the job at Lund Edwards. Complete her e-mail.

Dear Joanne,

Thanks for ¹giving me more details ² _____ the web designer job ³ _____ the phone. I would now ⁴ _____ to apply ⁵ _____ the job.

Please ⁶ _____ attached my CV. I'm available ⁷ _____ an interview ⁸ _____ any time.

I ⁹ _____ forward to hearing from you.

All ¹⁰ _____ wishes,

Lauren Charpentier

ON THE LINE **A** 12.1 Work in pairs. Student A looks at this page. Student B turns to page 153.

Student A

Lauren phones Joanne about her job application. Listen and complete the expressions that Joanne uses in the conversation.

This is *Joanne Samms.*

Oh, ...

Well, we've had a lot of applications. But yours is one of the most interesting. I was going to ...

Can you come to an interview here next week? How about ...

That's OK. You can leave her in our day care center ...

Come to the reception and ask for me. I'll come down ...

Me too. Bye ...

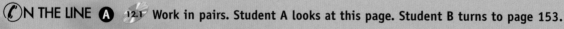
Your turn **B** Repeat the conversation. You are Joanne and Student B is Lauren.

Grammar

present perfect with *for* and *since*

How long have you worked as a freelancer?
***For** six years. / **Since** 2001.*

A Complete the rules by underlining the correct alternative.

With the present perfect, you use

| *for* with | a period of | time |
| | a point in | |

| *since* with | a period of | time |
| | a point in | |

B Write the questions and answers for a job interview. Put the verbs in brackets into the present perfect tense and choose *for* or *since*.

1 (live) in Vancouver – ten years

How long have you lived in Vancouver? – For ten years.

2 (be) a web designer – 1998

3 (work) for JPG – 3 years

4 (have) present job – 15 months

5 (study) French – last September

6 (be) a member of the Vancouver French Film Club – 6 months

■ More information:
Grammar review
and development
page 39
Grammar overview
page 100

▶ More practice:
Workbook pages
28 and 29

Speaking

A Work in pairs. Student A looks at this page. Student B turns to page 153.

Student A

You are Joanne Samms. Interview Lauren Charpentier for the job of web designer at Lund Edwards. You have lost her CV. Ask her to tell you where she was born.

Where were you born?

- where she went to school
- where she went to university
- what languages she speaks
- how many jobs she has had
- what she does now
- how long she has done this
- why she wants to work at Lund Edwards

Checklist ✓ job applications: *I would like to apply for the job. Please find attached my CV.* ✓ an invitation to an interview: *Can you come for an interview?* ✓ present perfect with *for* and *since*: *I've worked as a freelancer for eight years / since 1998.*

Grammar review and development 9–12

Comparatives and superlatives

	base form	comparative	superlative
one syllable	late, high	later, higher	latest, highest
two or more syllables	productive efficient	use 'more': more productive more efficient	use most: most productive most efficient
irregular	good, bad	better, worse	best, worst

A Look at the bar chart about production at a car plant and at the examples.

*Production was **higher** in October **than** in September – there was a three-week strike in September.*

*Our **best month** was October and our **worst month** was September.*

*Production **reached its highest point** in October – there were 22 working days that month.*

- More information: Grammar overview page 107
- More practice: Workbook page 30

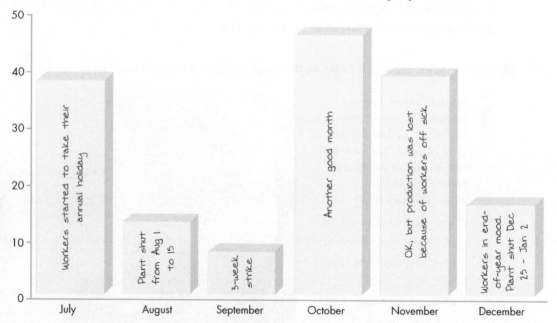

Your turn

B Now make three more statements about the chart.

must and should

Affirmative	Negative	Questions
I must ...	I shouldn't (should not) ...	Should I?
I should ...	I mustn't (must not) ...	Must I?

You use *must* and *should* to tell people what to do. *Must* is stronger than *should*.

You use *mustn't* (must not) and *shouldn't* (should not) to tell people what not to do. *Mustn't* is stronger than *shouldn't*.

A Read about the following situations at a car repair garage. Decide what things you should do and what things you shouldn't do. Talk about them using *must, should, mustn't* and *shouldn't.*

1 There is an accident in the car park and someone is badly injured.
- call an ambulance
- move the person
- cover them so they are warm

2 There is a problem with all the cars you have serviced because the mechanics haven't followed the car maker's instructions.
- tell customers to bring the product back for a free repair
- fire the mechanics
- say to the customers, 'These things happen. Can you bring back your car next week?'

3 An employee is stealing money from the company.
- tell the employee that you know about their activities
- call the police
- accuse the employee before you are sure of the facts

4 Customers bring their cars for servicing, but often the required parts haven't arrived because the parts department hasn't ordered them.
- improve the parts ordering system
- deny that there is a problem with the servicing
- fire the people in the parts department

5 The company is losing money.
- think that the company's money problems will just go away
- analyse why there are losses
- control costs

■ More information:
Grammar overview
page 102

▶ More practice:
Workbook page 27

B You are a young manager at the garage. Use the ideas in exercise A to ask your boss for advice about the different problems.

Someone in the car park is badly injured. Should I call an ambulance?

present perfect with *for* and *since*

Affirmative	Negative	Questions
You have worked.	You haven't (have not) worked.	Have you worked?

Lauren **has been** a freelancer *since 1998*.   She **has studied** *Spanish* **for 6 months**.

You can use the present perfect to talk about unfinished events. You can use it with the following time expressions:

- *since* + points in time.   ● *for* + periods of time.

A Write *for* or *since*.

1 since 2001   4 _____ 8 hours   7 _____ last November
2 _____ five years   5 _____ last year   8 _____ Monday last week
3 _____ five o'clock   6 _____ three months

B Complete the sentences with the present perfect forms of the verbs in brackets and *for* or *since*.

1 The Swedish company Stora has existed (exist) for over 700 years. It was founded in the 13th century.
2 Thomas Watson started IBM in 1924. It _____ (make) electronic computers _____ 1953.
3 Warren Buffet, the world's greatest investor, _____ (manage) Berkshire Hathaway _____ he left school.
4 General Motors _____ (be) the world's biggest car company _____ nearly 40 years.
5 People _____ (buy and sell) insurance at Lloyds of London _____ the middle of the seventeenth century.
6 Women _____ (wear) Chanel no. 5 _____ decades: it never goes out of fashion.

■ More information:
Grammar overview
page 100

● Verb list page 104

▶ More practice:
Workbook page 31

MODULE

4

NEW PRODUCTS, NEW MARKETS

This module looks at some new products and services and the secrets of their success. Two of the companies in the units are relatively new; two have been in existence for longer, but are innovating to reach new markets.

13 Low-cost airlines

Grammar	past simple with *ago*
Vocabulary	company development
On the line	changing a booking

> Do you like flying? Are there low-cost airlines operating in your country? Where do they fly to?

14 Bright ideas

Grammar	past continuous
Vocabulary	product development and finance
On the line	obtaining a meeting

> What's the secret for making and marketing a successful product? Why do most new business ideas fail?

15 Consumer electronics

Grammar	first conditional
Vocabulary	product features
On the line	negotiating an order
Writing	order confirmation

> What sort of gadgets do you have in your office or school, and at home? What's your favourite gadget?

16 Cosmetics and pharmaceuticals

Grammar	passive
Vocabulary	research, production and distribution
On the line	getting through

> Name some famous cosmetics brands. What are they each famous for?

♻ Grammar review and development 13–16

past simple with *ago*

past continuous

first conditional

passive

13 Low-cost airlines

Reading and speaking

A Read about easyJet's history.

1995
Stelios Ioannou ('Just call me Stelios') is bored with working at his father's shipping company in Athens. His father lends him £5 million and he launches EasyJet.

1997
easyJet starts services between Liverpool and Amsterdam. It chooses Liverpool as a base because it wants to use lower-cost airports.

1998
easyJet orders 15 brand-new Boeing Next Generation 737-700 aircraft with a list price of more than $500 million each.

2000
easyJet carries its 10 millionth passenger and sells its 4 millionth seat online.
Internet sales reach 85% of total sales.

2002
easyJet and Go merge to create Europe's number one low-cost airline.
Stelios leaves easyJet to concentrate on his easyCar car rental business.

B Talk about the events in the past simple.

Stelios launched easyJet in 1995.

C Work in pairs. Ask and answer questions in the past simple.

A: *Did Stelios launch easyJet in 1998?*
B: *No, he launched it in 1995.*

D Ask and answer questions with question words.

| when | why | how many | how much | ~~how old~~ |

A: *How old was Stelios when he launched easyJet?*
B: *He was ...*

Listening

A 13.1 A market researcher is interviewing four passengers about their experience of Quinnair, another new airline. In which order do they speak?

a a bank executive ___
c a retired person ___
b a supermarket worker ___
d a university teacher _1_

B Now listen again and complete the information in the table.

Traveller	Place coming from	Reason for trip	Fare paid	Satisfaction level*
University teacher	Nice			

*(7 = extremely satisfied, 1 = extremely dissatisfied)

Grammar past simple with *ago*

*Stelios **left** easyJet three years **ago**.*

$$\left.\begin{array}{l} When \\ How\ long\ ago \end{array}\right\}\ did\ easyJet\ carry\ its\ 10\ millionth\ passenger?$$

You can ask questions with
When ... ? or *How long ago ... ?*

A Complete the rules and the example.

You use the past simple with ___ago___
to talk about past events.
You put *ago* after a _____ of time.
This happened five years _____.

B Work in pairs. Student A looks at this
page. Student B turns to page 154.

Student A

Here are some more facts about easyJet.

Ask Student B questions with *How long ago ... ?* about events 1–3.

1 The Superbrand Council recognises easyJet as 'an outstanding brand name'.

How long ago did the Superbrand Council recognise easyJet as 'an outstanding brand name'?

2 Independent Television shows its first series (of five!) about easyJet.

3 The London Stock Exchange lists easyJet shares for the first time.

Now answer Student B's questions about events 4–6.

4 Sir Colin Chandler takes over as chairman. – 2001

5 EasyJet orders 120 aircraft from Airbus. – 2002

6 The first Airbus A319 goes into service. – 2003

■ More information:
Grammar review
and development
page 50
Grammar overview
page 99
▶ More practice:
Workbook page 32

ON THE LINE

A 13.2 Work in pairs. Student A looks at this page. Student B turns to page 154.

Student A

Rebecca phones Dawn at Quinnair to change her booking. Complete the expressions used by Dawn in the conversation.

Dawn speaking. How may I help?
What flight have you ...
Sorry, what ...
What's ...
Ah, here ....
Sorry, but all flights are ...
How about the 15th at 10.30 in the morning or ...
You're now booked on flight QZ345 leaving at ...
The fare is the same as on the flight you booked – £35. We need to ...

B Work in pairs. Practise the conversation.

Checklist

✓ past simple with *ago*:
*Stelios left easyJet five
years ago.*

✓ company development:
*Stelios founded easyJet in 1995.
It merged with Go in 2002.*

✓ change a booking:
I'd like to change my booking.

14 Bright ideas

Reading Ⓐ **Read about these new products.**

1 Akio Morita got the idea for the Walkman as he was flying across the Pacific.

2 Art Fry got the idea for Post-it notes while he was singing in church.

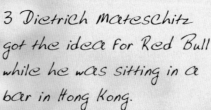

Post-it
Notes

3 Dietrich Mateschitz got the idea for Red Bull while he was sitting in a bar in Hong Kong.

Ⓑ **Now match sentences a–c to the background information below.**

a The pieces of paper in his book kept falling out. ___

b There he saw the 'tonic drinks' that are very popular in Asia. ___

c The flight was very long and he was bored. _1_

Grammar **past continuous**

*He **was sitting** in a bar when he had an idea.*

Ⓐ **Complete the rules.**

You use the past continuous to talk about something that was in progress when something else _____.
You form the past continuous with *was/were* and the _____ form of the verb.

Ⓑ **There was a big power cut in Sydney last year. Complete what these people say about what they were doing when it happened. Use the correct forms of the verbs in brackets.**

1 I __was going__ (go) home on the train when it __stopped__ (stop) in a tunnel.

2 We _____ (eat) at a restaurant when the lights _____ (go) out.

3 I _____ (watch) a film at a cinema when the screen _____ (go) black.

4 I _____ (take) a lift when it suddenly _____ (get stuck) between floors.

5 We _____ (listen) to music on a battery radio at home when they _____ (interrupt) the programme.

6 I _____ (have) beer in a bar when everything _____ (go) dark and everyone _____ (cheer).

■ More information:
Grammar review
and development
page 50
Grammar overview
page 100
▶ More practice:
Workbook page 34

ON THE LINE **A** 🔊 **14.1** **Listen to the conversation and answer the questions.**

1 What does Clara Rios do?   *She's a professor of chemistry.*
2 What has she developed?
3 Why does she want a meeting with BAF Venture Capital?
4 Has Clara met Jane Anderson before?
5 When do they arrange to meet?

B 🔊 **14.2** **Listen again to the second half of the conversation. Complete the sentences.**

Clara: *If we can meet, I can tell you more about it. I'm going to be in New York next week.*
Jane: *Next week's ...   How about ...*
Clara: *Well, I could stay over ...*
Jane: *OK... How about Monday 25th at 2? I can see you ...*
Clara: *Fine. Half an hour ...*
Jane: *Do you know where we are? BAF Venture Capital is on Madison Avenue and 39th Street – 600 Madison Avenue. Come up to the tenth floor and ask ...*
Clara: *OK. See you there on Monday at 2 pm. Thank you so much! I'm sure ...*

Your turn **C** **Work in pairs. A phones B to get an appointment to discuss a product.**

Student A: You have a new product that you want to finance (think of something).

Student B: You work for a venture capital company.

A: *If we can meet, I can tell you more about it.*
B: *How about ...*

Vocabulary and speaking **A** **Use the expressions in the box to complete the commentary.**

business plan
~~ingredients~~
manufacturing
consumers
plant
industrial secret
marketing
start-up capital
investors

You think of a new food or drink product. Perhaps its [1] ~~ingredients~~ – the things it's made of – are an [2] _____ _____. But there's a big difference between making something in your kitchen and [3] _____ it in large quantities in a [4] _____! And there's a big difference between selling through local shops and [5] _____ the product to millions of [6] _____. To develop and market the product you need [7] _____ _____, perhaps from a bank or from [8] _____. You go to these investors and you show them your [9] _____ _____ – how much you want to invest in your business, how much profit you expect to make, etc.

B **Work in pairs. Student A looks at this page. Student B looks at page 154.**

Student A
You are Jane Anderson at BAF Venture Capital. You meet Clara Rios (Student B) to discuss her plans for the new energy drink.

• Ask about the exact ingredients of the drink.
  What exactly is your drink made of?

• Ask Clara how much start-up capital she needs.

• Ask about Clara's plans to manufacture, market and distribute it.

• You think that a sales figure of 10 million cans in the first year is unrealistic, and that a price of $1.50 is too expensive, especially in Latin America. The profit of 10 per cent per can is unrealistically high.

• Suggest more realistic figures and work out the new profit (or loss!) figure.

Checklist	✔ past continuous:	✔ arrange a meeting:	✔ production and finance:
	He was sitting in a bar when he had an idea.	*Half an hour should be enough. You won't regret it.*	*business plan, investors, start-up capital ...*

15 Consumer electronics

Reading and vocabulary

A Read the advertisement.

 iPod

The super-slim iPod defines what a digital music player should be. **1** It's lighter than two CDs, can **2** hold up to 10,000 songs and thousands of digital photos, and works as a personal voice recorder. Now you can download with iTunes for Mac and Windows **3** at blazing speeds, and take your entire music collection with you wherever you go. Available for Mac and Windows **4** starting at $299.

15GB, 20GB and 40GB Models

At **5** just over half an inch thick, the iPod **6** fits comfortably in the palm of your hand and slips easily into your pocket – and your life. **7** Merely 5.6 ounces, it weighs less than two Compact Discs, and even many cell phones. And yet the iPod gives you **8** a huge 15GB, 20GB or 40GB hard drive – big enough to hold 10,000 songs. Do the math: that's four weeks of music – played continuously, 24/7 – or **9** one new song a day for the next 27 years.

The iTunes Music Store. Now for Mac and Windows.

Build a collection of music on your iPod with songs downloaded from the iTunes Music Store. Choose from hundreds of thousands of songs you can preview and buy with just one click. The iTunes Music Store stays open 24/7 – right on your Mac or Windows PC. Within a minute of finding a song you like, you can own it. You can make unlimited playlists, burn individual songs to CD as many times as you like and **10** take all your music on your iPod wherever you go.

B Work in pairs. Match the underlined expressions to the iPod's characteristics.

a size _5_   **c** speed ___   **e** capacity (how much it can hold) ___
b weight ___   **d** price ___

C Now match the expressions in the box to a–e.

1 weighs a ton _b_	**3** high-speed ___	**5** light ___	**7** low-cost ___
2 slow ___	**4** expensive ___	**6** gigantic ___	**8** miniature ___

Listening and speaking

A 🎵 **15.1** Listen to these four conversations at the Consumer Electronics Show in Las Vegas. Match the expressions in the conversations to *a*, *b* or *c*.

a the 'small talk' when they meet
travel to Las Vegas ___
health _1_
work ___
family ___

b the product they talk about
plasma screens ___
games consoles ___
DVD players ___
digital cameras ___

c what they are going to do next
make a phone call ___
go back to company's stand ___
have lunch with a supplier ___
listen to Bill Gates's speech ___

Your turn

B Work in pairs. You and an old friend meet at a trade show. Use the outlines to start conversations with some small talk. Then continue them.

1 **A:** Hi, _____, how are you?
   B: Fine. I had the flu last week, but I'm OK now. And you?
   A: Fine, ...

2 **A:** Hello, _____.
   B: Oh, hi, _____.
   A: Didn't think I'd see you here. How are you?
   B: A bit tired. I ....

3 **E:** Hey, _____, nice to see you!
   F: Good to see *you*, _____.
   E: How's your family?
   F: Fine, ...

4 **A:** Ah, _____, good to see you! How's business?
   B: Great to see you, _____. Business is ...

Grammar first conditional

*If you buy 200,000 units, the unit price **will be** $19.*

You use the first conditional to talk about situations which are possible if a condition is fulfilled.

You form the first conditional with the present simple tense in the if-clause and *will* in the main clause.

A **Complete the sentences with the correct forms of the verbs in brackets.**

1 If you <u>order</u> (order) 300,000 units, we <u>'ll reduce</u> (reduce) the unit price to $17.

2 If we _____ (deliver) 400,000 over 3 years, the price _____ (be) even lower.

3 If I _____ (give) you a lower price, I _____ (lose) money.

4 If we _____ (reach) an agreement today, my personal assistant _____ (fax) the contract this evening.

5 If you _____ (come) to Shanghai, I _____ (show) you all the sights.

6 If you _____ (go) to a competitor, I _____ (not be) happy.

■ More information:
Grammar review
and development
page 51
Grammar overview
page 103

▶ More practice:
Workbook page 36

ON THE LINE **A** **15.2 Listen to the conversation and complete the information about Ellmart's order for DVD players.**

Quantity: <u>200,000 units</u>

Delivery period: _____ _____

Unit price: _____ _____

Your turn **B** **Student A looks at this page. Student B turns to page 155.**

Student A

You are Henry Steen. Lee Peng (Student B) calls you to discuss your order for DVD players. Start the conversation as in exercise A above.

A: *Henry Steen here.*

B: *Hello, Henry, this is Lee Peng in Shanghai.*

A: *Hello, Mr Lee. I was expecting your call. How are you?*

- Then find out prices for the following quantities and delivery periods.
  300,000 units over 2 years: _____
  400,000 units over 3 years: _____

- Try to negotiate lower prices for these two periods.
  If we order ... , can you reduce the unit price further?

- Come to an agreement.
  OK. We'll start by ordering ... I'll confirm our order in writing, of course.

- Find out the payment terms.
  What are your normal payment terms?

- Accept Lee Peng's invitation politely.

- End the conversation suitably.

Writing

Write the e-mail that Henry Steen sends to Lee Peng to confirm his order. Use the terms that you agreed to in Your turn.

Dear Mr Lee,

It was good to talk to you today. This is to confirm ...

Checklist

✓ product features:
slim, light, slips easily into your pocket ...

✓ first conditional:
If you order more, the price will be lower

✓ negotiate an order:
I was expecting your call. We're interested in going ahead with ...

✓ confirm an order:
unit price, payment terms ...

16 Cosmetics and pharmaceuticals

Speaking **A** Work in pairs. Student A looks at this page. **Student B turns to page 155.**

Student A

Ask B for the missing information in this website.

What are Avon's annual sales?

AVON	
Annual sales:	$ _____
Markets:	Avon sells its products in _____ countries
Distribution:	3.9 million direct sales representatives
Product lines:	Avon Color _____ _____ Avon Bath & Body _____ _____ Avon Wellness _____ _____ becoming _____ mark.(TM) _____

Vocabulary and listening

A Match the expressions to their meanings.

1 direct selling
2 distribution channel
3 manufacturing plant
4 production
5 R and D
6 raw materials
7 outside supplier

a a particular way of moving products from a producer to consumers
b when products are sold direct to consumers, rather than through shops
c developing new products
d a company that provides products and services to another company
e the things that products are made of
f the place where products are made
g making products

B **16.1** Listen to an interview with a cosmetics industry expert. In which order do you hear the expressions 1 – 7 above? 2, _____

ON THE LINE **A** 16.2 **Listen to different people phoning a pharmaceuticals company, ZRC. Which department does the receptionist put each caller through to?**

a press office ____

b marketing _1_

c research and development ____

d human resources ____

B **Write in which conversation you hear each expression.**

a How may I direct your call? _1_

b Can I speak to someone who deals with ... ____

c What's the purpose of your call? ____

d Who may I say is calling? ____

e I'm trying to reach ... ____

f The number's unobtainable. ____

g May I speak to someone in ... ____

h What is your call concerning? ____

Your turn **C** **Work in pairs. Student A looks at this page. Student B turns to page 155.**

Student A

You are the receptionist at ZRC. Student B is a caller. Use the information below to ask and answer questions.

• Answer the phone. *ZRC, good morning/afternoon.*

• Ask why B is calling

• Say you are connecting B

Grammar

passive

*The products **are sold b**y sales reps.*

You use the passive to talk about something affected by an action.

*Research **is done** at the research centre.*

You form the present simple of the passive with *is/are* + past participle of the verb.

*A new plant **was buil**t in 2003.*

You form the past simple of the passive with *was/were* + past participle of the verb.

A **Rewrite the sentences in the passive. Start with *Its ...***

1 Avon sells its products in department stores.
Its products are sold in department stores.

2 Avon markets its products all over the world.

3 Avon manufactures its products in its own plants.

4 Avon built its Russian manufacturing plant in 2003.

5 Avon opened a new research centre in New York State in 2004.

■ More information:
Grammar review
and development
page 51
Grammar overview
page 102

▶ More practice:
Workbook page 39

Checklist

✓ passive:
*The products are distributed
by direct sales representatives.*

✓ production and distribution:
*direct selling, distribution
channel, R & D ...*

✓ put people through to the right
department: *How may I direct
your call?*

Grammar review and development 13–16

past simple with ago

*Stelios **founded** easyJet nearly x years **ago**.*

You use the past simple with *ago* to talk about past events.
You use *ago* after a period of time.

(A) Look at the information about Ryanair. Ask questions about the airline and answer with *ago*.

1 Ryanair started its Dublin-London route. (1986)
   A: *When did Ryanair start its Dublin-London route?*
   B: *Nearly x years ago.*

2 It listed its shares on the Dublin stock exchange. (1996)

3 It ordered 45 planes from Boeing. (1998)

4 It launched its website. (2000)

5 It opened Frankfurt-Hahn as its second European base. (2002)

6 It took over Buzz airline from KLM. (2003)

■ More information: Grammar overview page 99

(B) Now ask the same questions using *How long ago did ... ?*

▶ More practice: Workbook page 40

1 *How long ago did Ryanair start on the Dublin-London route?*

past continuous

Affirmative	Negative	Questions
I was day-dreaming.	I wasn't day-dreaming.	Was I day-dreaming?

*I **was day-dreaming** when the boss walked into my office.*
*They **were taking** the lift when there was a power cut.*

You use the past continuous to talk about something that was in progress when something else happened.
You form the past continuous with *was/were* and the *–ing* form of the verb.

(A) Complete the sentences with the correct forms of the verbs in brackets.

1 I <u>was writing</u> (write) the business plan when my computer _____ (crash) and I lost 50 pages.

2 I _____ (go) to see a venture capital company when I _____ (hear) it was bankrupt.

3 We _____ (prepare) to launch the product when there _____ (be) a fire in the factory.

4 Sales _____ (rise) fast when our sales manager _____ (leave) the company.

■ More information: Grammar overview page 100

5 We _____ (get into) the Asian market when there _____ (be) a financial crash there.

6 I _____ (talk) to a possible client when I _____ (find out) they had already signed with a competitor.

first conditional

*If you **order** today, we **will deliver** next week.*

You use the first conditional to talk about situations which are possible if a condition is fulfilled.

You form the first conditional with the present simple tense in the if-clause and *will* in the main clause.

Ⓐ Match the sentences to the person or organisation (a–f) that says them.

1 If you don't repay the loan on time, we will take your house and sell it.

2 If your share price keeps falling, I'll sell my shares.

3 If you deliver late once more, we won't order from you again.

4 If your machinery is dangerous, we'll close your factory.

5 If you don't tell us exactly what you want, we can't let you have it.

6 If you correct the information in your advertisements, we won't investigate further.

a the advertising authorities

b a bank

c a factory inspector

d a supplier

e an investor

f a customer

first conditional: *unless*

***Unless** you repay the loan on time, we will take your house and sell it.*
If you don't repay the loan on time, we will take your house and sell it.

***Unless** your share price starts to rise, I'll sell my shares.*
If your share price keeps falling, I'll sell my shares.

You can use *unless* to replace if + a negative expression.

■ More information:
Grammar overview
page 103

▶ More practice:
Workbook page 40

Ⓑ Rewrite sentences 3–6 using *unless*. (The second part of the sentence should stay the same.)

passive

*The products **are sold** by sales reps.*
You use the passive to talk about something affected by an action.

*Research **is done** at the research centre.*
You form the present simple of the passive with *is/are* + past participle of the verb.

*A new plant **was built** in 2003.*
You form the past simple of the passive with *was/were* + past participle of the verb.

Ⓐ Rewrite the sentences as shown.

1 DeBeers mines gold in South Africa.
Gold is mined by DeBeers in South Africa.

2 Refiners transform the ore into pure gold.

3 They sell the gold on international markets.

4 Jewellers buy gold.

5 Specialist workers turn the gold into jewellery.

6 Retailers sell the most expensive jewellery in streets such as Bond Street in London.

7 Rich and not-so-rich people buy it.

■ More information:
Grammar overview
page 102

▶ More practice:
Workbook page 40

Ⓑ Now ask questions about 1–7 above using *Who ... ?*

1 *Who is gold mined by?*

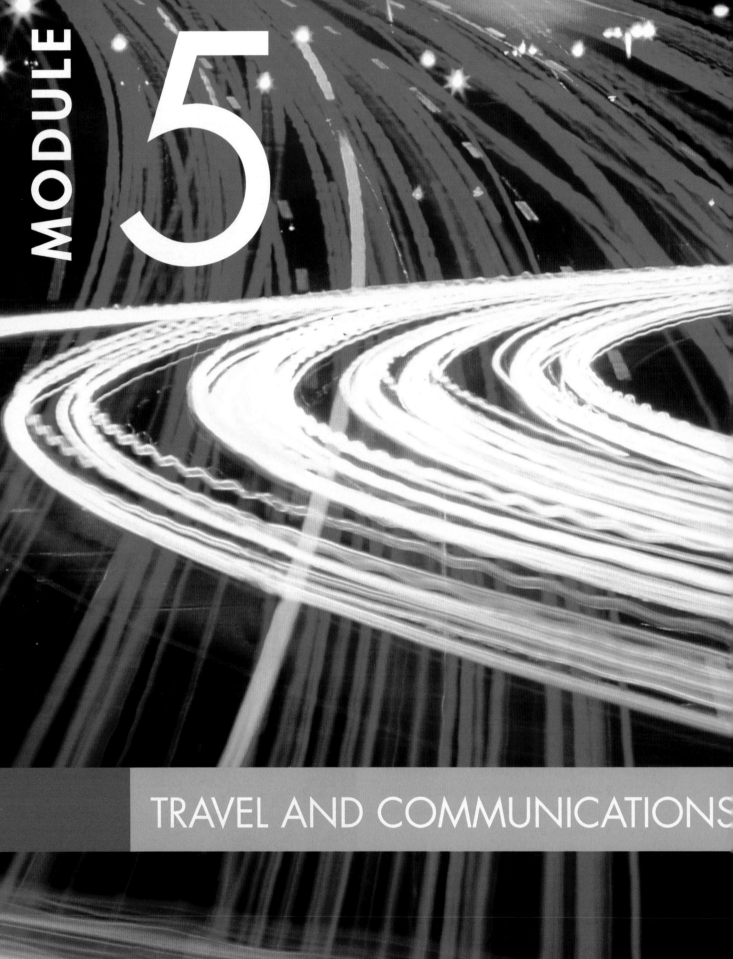

TRAVEL AND COMMUNICATIONS

This module looks at some of the problems of people travelling to work, and asks if people need to travel at all in order to work or to have meetings.

17 I'm running late

Grammar	second conditional
Vocabulary	traffic and jams; adjective opposites
On the line	delays

> What is public transport like in your area? Do you use it?

18 Are you considerate?

Grammar	*should/shouldn't*
Vocabulary	driving adjectives
On the line	saying you phoned earlier

> What sort of driver are you? If you don't drive, what annoys you most about other people's driving?

19 New ways of working

| Vocabulary | remote working; trends |
| On the line | mobile phone problems |

> Why do offices exist? Why doesn't everyone work from home?

20 Why travel?

Grammar	verbs with prepositions and particles
On the line	a conference call
Writing	a follow-up e-mail

> Why do people go to face-to-face meetings? Why don't they just use video-conferencing all the time?

♻ Grammar review and development 17–20

second conditional

should/shouldn't

verbs with prepositions and particles

53

17 I'm running late

Reading and vocabulary

A Read this article.

The most noticeable thing about the recent 'Paris sans Voiture' day (Paris without cars) was the number of cars on the roads. Cars everywhere, stuck in traffic jams as all around the city drivers refused to abandon their Renaults and Peugeots. Part of the centre of the city was sealed off to all private cars — taxis, buses and emergency services were allowed, but nobody else.

But the idea of going one day in 365 without a car caused anger among many Parisians. Some café and restaurant owners shut down for the day. 'We've opened anyway, but a lot of others haven't as there'll be no customers if there are no cars,' one café owner explained to me.

And yet Paris has some of the best public transport of any city I have ever lived in or visited. The Paris metro is extremely efficient — a train on the busiest lines every 3 or 4 minutes at least, the lines criss-crossing the whole of the capital and intersecting with the regional urban railway network, which can zoom travellers from the city centre to Paris's airports in under 45 minutes.

Likewise, Paris buses are among the most modern, comfortable forms of public transport, again, frequent and reliable — and, like the metro, incredibly cheap. Paris public transport is heavily subsidised by high taxes. And yet, at rush hour, there are long tailbacks in the narrow streets of the city centre, caused by parking cars and daytime van deliveries.

So what are the Paris authorities doing to improve life for Paris commuters and residents? Paris's Mayor, Bertrand Delanoë, has already done a lot to help, says bus passenger Laura Pierre. 'He has introduced bus lanes and more cycle lanes, and has made sure the police enforce them with heavy fines for anyone caught in them illegally,' she says. 'Before, no one took any notice so the buses were really slow. Now it's much better.'

Others say that he needs to do more. 'If car drivers had to pay to come into central Paris, like they do in London, there would be less traffic,' said one person I spoke to.

B Match the words in the article to the adjectives that describe them.

1 streets	a cheap
	b comfortable
	c efficient
2 buses	d frequent
	e modern
3 public transport in general	f narrow
	g reliable
4 the metro	h subsidised

C Now match the adjectives a–h to their opposites.

1 wide _f_ 　　　　　5 out-dated ___
2 unsubsidised ___ 　　6 infrequent ___
3 unreliable ___ 　　　7 inefficient ___
4 uncomfortable ___ 　　8 expensive ___

Your turn

D Use the adjectives and their opposites above to talk about traffic and public transport in your area.

The buses in this city are cheap and efficient.

> (!) 16 km/h is the average speed of cars in Paris
> 1.7 billion hours are spent every year in traffic jams by the UK workforce.
> In many cities, 50% of air pollution comes from transport.

Grammar **second conditional**

*If there **was** a day 'without cars' in your area, **would** you stay at home?*
- Yes, I would. / No, I wouldn't. I'd cycle to work.

You use the second conditional to talk about situations that are possible but not likely to happen.

You form the second conditional with the past simple tense in the if-clause and *would* in the main clause.

A **Work in pairs. Ask and answer questions about transport with the correct forms of the verbs in brackets.**

1 public transport (is) free, (use) it more?

   A: *If public transport was free, would you use it more?*

   B: *Yes, I would. / No, I'd still use my car.*

2 car tax (double), (sell) your car?

3 your journey to work (take) more than two hours, (move) nearer to work?

4 you (have) to pay to drive into the city centre, (use) public transport?

■ More information:
Grammar review
and development
page 62
Grammar overview
page 103

▶ More practice:
Workbook page 42

B **Now talk about your partner.**

If public transport was free, ... wouldn't use it more. He/she would still drive to work.

ON THE LINE **A** 🔊 17.1 **Complete the information about each of the three conversations.**

	City	Reason for journey	Problem
1	Paris	meeting	stuck in traffic
2			
3			

B **Listen again. In which conversation do you hear each of these expressions?**

It's running half an hour late. ____

I'm stuck in a jam. 1

Go ahead without me. ____

I've been held up. ____

I'll be with you in an hour. ____

Can you tell him I've been delayed, please? ____

Your turn

C **Work in pairs. Student A looks at this page. Student B turns to page 156.**

 Student A

Take the role of each of the people waiting in the situations above. React as shown when the person you are waiting for (Student B) arrives.

Conversation 1: You are Maggie waiting for Alain. Say you are glad that he made it.

Maggie: *Hi Alain. I'm glad you made it.*

Alain: *I'm glad to be here. I had a terrible journey.*

• Ask him if he found somewhere to park.

• Ask him if he still refuses to take the metro.

Conversation 2: You are Mehmet waiting for Cathy. Say hello and say you are glad she made it.

• Ask her why the ferry was late.

• Ask her what she would like to drink.

Conversation 3: You are the receptionist waiting for Anthea.

• Tell her that she is an hour late and that Mr Randall has had to cancel the appointment.

• Tell her to come back tomorrow at 10.

Checklist ✓ traffic and jams:
commuter, traffic, tailback, public transport, metro ...

✓ adjective opposites:
frequent/infrequent, reliable/unreliable ...

✓ second conditional:
If fares rose by 50 per cent, I'd use my car.

✓ apologise:
Sorry I'm late. I was stuck in a jam.

18 Are you considerate?

A Work in pairs. Find the three things that annoy you most about public transport.

QUESTIONNAIRE

Are you a commuter?

What's the worst thing about public transport? People who ...

1 get onto trains before passengers have time to get off

2 shout into their mobile phones

3 put their feet on the seat opposite them

4 eat smelly food

5 use loud 'personal' stereos

6 drop litter

7 put their bags on the seat next to them when there are people standing

8 play musical instruments on trains and ask you for money

Grammar

should/shouldn't

People **should** talk on their mobiles quietly. They **shouldn't** talk so loudly.

You can use *should* and *shouldn't* (*should not*) to talk about obligation, for example, about people's proper behaviour. *Should* and *shouldn't* are not as strong as *must*.

You **should** leave a tip of about 10 per cent in restaurants.

You can also use *should/shouldn't* to give advice.

Compare with:

You **don't have to tip** waiters = You **needn't tip** waiters—service is included. But you can leave a euro or two if the waiter has been especially helpful.

You can use *don't have to / needn't* to talk about actions or activities which are not obligatory.

If we leave at 12 we **should be** there by 2.

You can also use *should* to talk about things that will probably happen.

A Use the points from the questionnaire above to say what people should or shouldn't do. If possible, say one sentence with *should* and one with *shouldn't*.

1 *People should wait for passengers to get off before they get onto trains.*
People shouldn't get onto trains before passengers have time to get off.

B Match the two parts of these sentences.

1 If they post the letter 1st class today,

2 Hit that button

3 Study hard

4 If you go straight down here,

5 Prepare the presentation well

6 If you explain things clearly,

a and the light should come on.

b and you should pass the exam.

c I should get it tomorrow.

d they should see your point of view.

e you should see the post office on your right.

f and it should go ok.

■ More information: Grammar review and development page 102
Grammar overview page 63

▶ More practice: Workbook page 44

ON THE LINE **A** 🔘 18.1 **Helen phones Rebecca. Which two expressions do you hear?**

1 there was no answer ____
2 the line was busy ____

3 your voice-mail was on ____
4 you were in a meeting ____

B 🔘 18.2 **Then Rebecca talks about her journey to work. Which three problems from the questionnaire above does she mention?**

a 4   b ____   c ____

Your turn

C **Work in pairs. Phone a colleague. Say what happened when you phoned earlier. Then continue the conversation.**

Student A: Talk about your difficult journey to work because of one of the points in the questionnaire above.
Student B: Sympathise and agree. Say what people should or shouldn't do.

A: *Hello.*
B: *Hello, … I phoned you earlier, but the line went dead.*
A: *Yes, I'm having a lot of trouble with my phone.*
B: *How are things?*
A: *Well, my journey into work was a nightmare. I don't know if I can go on with this much longer.*
B: *What happened?*

Vocabulary and speaking

A **Match the expressions in italics to their meanings.**

1 I don't mind *commuting* by car. It gives me a chance to think and listen to music.

2 *Carpooling* is a very good idea. You get to share costs and there are fewer cars on the road.

3 They talk about *road rage* in the newspapers, but in my experience, drivers are very considerate.

4 I think *reserved lanes* are a waste of time – they're always empty, and the other lanes are very crowded.

5 The *rush* used to last an hour or two in the morning, and the same in the evening, but now it lasts most of the day!

a when you share your car with others, who may pay part of the cost

b travelling a long distance to work

c a part of the road that is reserved for buses, taxis or people who are carpooling

d one of the times of day when traffic is heaviest – *rush hour*

e violence and angry behaviour between car drivers

B **Now give your opinion about what the people said.**

I hate commuting by car, and the public transport is terrible. It would be good to live in the city centre near where I work, but there are no houses with gardens.

C **Complete this table, provide more words and use them to talk about your driving style.**

noun	adjective	adverb
courtesy	courteous	courteously
	aggressive	
		considerately

Checklist   ✓ *should/shouldn't:*
People shouldn't put their feet on the seats.

✓ *driving nouns and adjectives:*
aggression/aggressive, safety/safe …

✓ *say you couldn't reach someone:*
Your voice-mail was on.

57

19 New ways of working

Reading and vocabulary

A Read the article.

THE VALUE REPORT

Remote working
Staff benefit from remote working trend

IT IS A WELL-KNOWN FACT that happy employees make happy customers. But how do you keep staff happy when they're fighting the transport system twice a day or having to deal with family commitments?

The growth of mobile technologies is changing the culture of how and where we work. In the UK, an estimated 400,000 new people every year take advantage of flexible working, and at least 2.2 million use technology to work away from the office, according to government figures. The result is more opportunities for people with families, less pressure on the transport system, and a better chance for staff to find a work-life balance.

There are four types of remote working:

- Travelling workers, such as engineers, move around as part of their job and use laptops connected to the internet via mobile phone networks.

- 'Day extenders' do part of their work from home in addition to their day in the office. Typically these are more senior executives who catch up on e-mail in the evening using their home internet connection.

- 'Campus workers' are often found at large industrial organisations. Perhaps they never leave the site, but they are often not at their desk and will use mobile devices to work and communicate.

- Teleworkers work from home one or more days per week. They increasingly rely on broadband connections to access corporate data.

Adapted from Computing – UK, 11 Sept 2003 (Sarah Arnott)

B Match expressions 1–6 to their definitions (a–f).

1 remote working
2 flexible working
3 work-life balance
4 broadband connection
5 laptop
6 mobile devices

a the amount of time you spend working in relation to the amount of time not working, being with your family, etc.
b working away from a normal office
c working in different places at different times, not at normal office hours
d phones, handheld computers, etc.
e fast access to the internet
f a small portable computer, also called a 'notebook'

Your turn > **C** What are the advantages and problems of working away from a normal office?
Could you do your work, or part of it, as one of the following?

a travelling worker **b** day extender **c** campus worker **d** teleworker

eaking and vocabulary

Ⓐ Work in pairs. Student A looks at this page. Student B looks at page 156.

Student A

Ask Student B for the missing information about trends in Europe.

How many mobile phone users are there in Europe now?

- Then answer Student B's questions.

	Five years ago	Now	In five years
Mobile phones	200 million		510 million
Homes with broadband		90 million	
Teleworkers	35 million		125 million

Ⓑ Look at the expressions used for talking about trends.

The number of { mobile phone users **has increased** *from 200 million to 380 million.*

homes with broadband **has gone up** *from 10 million to 90 million.*

teleworkers **is going to rise** *from 80 million today to 125 million in five years.*

Your turn **Ⓒ** Talk about the numbers in the table in the same way.

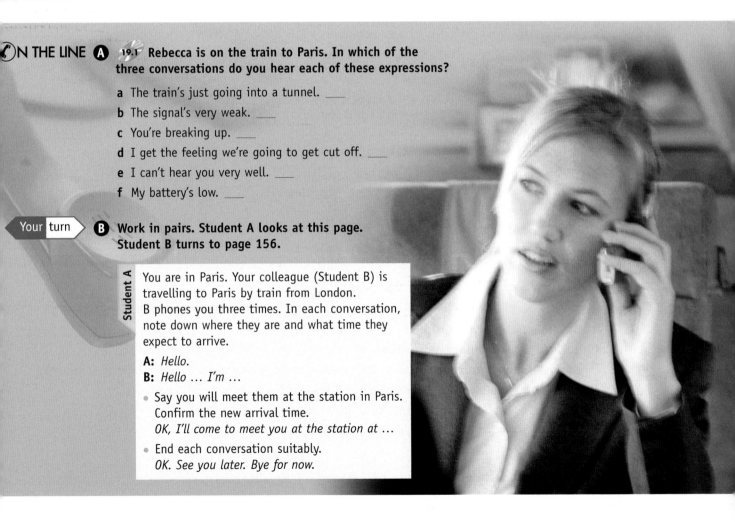

ON THE LINE **Ⓐ** 🔊 19.1 Rebecca is on the train to Paris. In which of the three conversations do you hear each of these expressions?

a The train's just going into a tunnel. ___

b The signal's very weak. ___

c You're breaking up. ___

d I get the feeling we're going to get cut off. ___

e I can't hear you very well. ___

f My battery's low. ___

Your turn **Ⓑ** Work in pairs. Student A looks at this page. Student B turns to page 156.

Student A

You are in Paris. Your colleague (Student B) is travelling to Paris by train from London.
B phones you three times. In each conversation, note down where they are and what time they expect to arrive.

A: *Hello.*

B: *Hello ... I'm ...*

- Say you will meet them at the station in Paris. Confirm the new arrival time.
OK, I'll come to meet you at the station at ...

- End each conversation suitably.
OK. See you later. Bye for now.

✓ remote working: *teleworker, broadband ...*

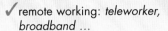 ✓ trends: *increase, go up, rise*

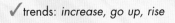 ✓ mobile phone expressions: *You're breaking up.*

20 Why travel?

'A video-conferencing suite'.

'A webcam'.

Listening and speaking

A 🔵 20.1 **Professor Paul Bremner is an expert on video-conferencing. Listen to the interview with him and answer the questions by completing the statements.**

1 Why do companies use video-conferencing?

   Companies can save a lot of __time__ and __money__ when managers don't have to travel to meetings.

2 Why isn't video-conferencing more popular?

   There are _____ reasons and there are also the human _____.

3 Why are webcams not used more?

   They are _____ but they are not always easy to _____ _____. They are good for _____-_____-_____ communication, but if you have a number of people in different places, you really need a _____-_____ _____.

4 What are the pros and cons of video-conferencing?

   The cost is _____ _____, and the _____ _____ is getting very good. You just _____ _____ the room, _____ _____ and _____ _____ the equipment. But the _____ in the room must be exactly right.

5 What are the human factors?

   Meetings can be rather _____. You need a good _____, and if someone wants to speak, they should _____ their hand _____ first.

Grammar

verbs with prepositions and particles

*We **went into** the room and **sat down**.*

*The cost of the equipment is **coming down**.*

The prepositions and particles that follow some verbs sometimes help to clarify or intensify their meaning.

*Your radio's too loud – can you **turn down** the sound, please?*

*Your radio's too loud – can you **turn** the sound **down**, please?*

Sometimes, the object can be placed between the verb and the particle.

*The plane **took off**.*

Verbs followed by particles that change their meaning can be called phrasal verbs.

A **Match the two parts of the sentences containing verbs with prepositions and particles.**

- More information:
  Grammar review
  and development
  page 63
  Grammar overview
  page 104
- More practice:
  Workbook page 49

1 There was a transport strike in Paris,   a you're breaking up.

2 Listen to the conversation and   b note down what you hear.

3 I can't hear you: c so some cafés shut down for the day.

4 I was held up   d in slow-moving traffic.

5 Wait for other people to get off   e the bus before you get on.

⊘N THE LINE **A** 🔊 **20.2** **Keith, Alain and Daljit are having a conference call about the Crazy Raiders video game that we saw in Module 1. Which alternative expressions in italics do you hear? (Both expressions are acceptable.)**

1 Can you *hang/hold* on while I get Daljit in Bangalore?

2 I've got Alain in Paris on the *line/phone* for our conference call.

3 Right, as I *said / was saying* at our meeting in London, ...

4 Alain, can you *say / tell us* more about this?

5 Daljit, would you like to *say something / come in* here?

6 Can you both calm down a *minute / moment*!

Your turn **B** **Work in threes. Student A looks at this page. Student B and Student C turn to page 157.**

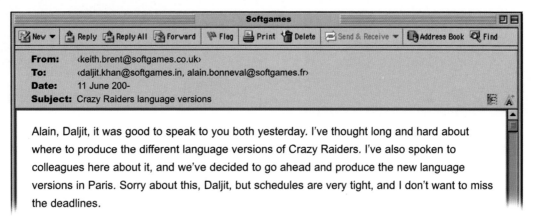

Student A

You are the boss of a new low-cost airline called SmartJet. You want to produce some cheap newspaper advertising for newspapers in French, German and Italian. You think your marketing director, Bernie (Student B) can write the advertisements. However, you are also considering the idea of using an advertising agency in Berlin run by Chris (Student C). As Bernie is on a business trip to Madrid, you have organised a three-way conference call to discuss the project.

Ask Bernie and Chris to talk about the possibilities, costs, etc. Use some of the call management expressions above.

Writing **A** **Read the e-mail that Keith sent after the conference call.**

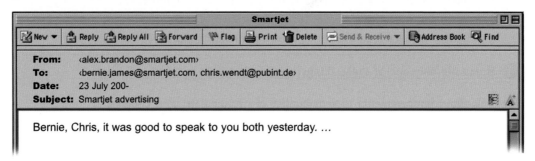

```
                              Softgames
 New ▾ | Reply  Reply All  Forward | Flag | Print  Delete | Send & Receive ▾ | Address Book  Find

 From:    ‹keith.brent@softgames.co.uk›
 To:      ‹daljit.khan@softgames.in, alain.bonneval@softgames.fr›
 Date:    11 June 200-
 Subject: Crazy Raiders language versions

 Alain, Daljit, it was good to speak to you both yesterday. I've thought long and hard about
 where to produce the different language versions of Crazy Raiders. I've also spoken to
 colleagues here about it, and we've decided to go ahead and produce the new language
 versions in Paris. Sorry about this, Daljit, but schedules are very tight, and I don't want to miss
 the deadlines.
```

B **Now write an e-mail following your conference call in On the line above. Write to the other two participants about what you discussed, what you decided and what you think of the decision.**

```
                              Smartjet
 New ▾ | Reply  Reply All  Forward | Flag | Print  Delete | Send & Receive ▾ | Address Book  Find

 From:    ‹alex.brandon@smartjet.com›
 To:      ‹bernie.james@smartjet.com, chris.wendt@pubint.de›
 Date:    23 July 200-
 Subject: Smartjet advertising

 Bernie, Chris, it was good to speak to you both yesterday. ...
```

Checklist
✓ verbs with prepositions and particles: *Listen to the conversation and note down what you hear.*

✓ conference call expressions: *Can you hold on while I get Bernie in Madrid?*

✓ follow-up expressions: *It was good to speak to you yesterday.*

second conditional

*If you **had** to pay to drive into the centre, **would** you **use** public transport?*
*– Yes, I **would**. / No, I **wouldn't**. **I'd take** my car anyway.*

You use the second conditional to talk about situations that are possible but not likely to happen.

You form the first conditional with the past simple tense in the if-clause and *would* in the main clause.

Ⓐ If you were the Minister for Employment in your country, what would you do to improve the working conditions of ordinary people?

Would you ...

1 raise the minimum wage?
   I wouldn't raise the minimum wage. It's already too high for a lot of companies.
2 reduce the number of working hours per week?
3 increase the number of weeks of paid holiday?
4 increase the length of parental leave when people have children?
5 force companies to have crèches for employees with children?
6 subsidise broadband internet access so more people could work from home?

Ⓑ If you did only one of these things: what would it be?

Ⓒ Talk about improvements to your quality of life. Explain your choices.

If you could ...

1 live anywhere, where would it be?
   I'd live in a big house in the country, miles from the nearest village.
2 work (more) from home, would you do this? Why / why not?
3 make one big improvement to your home, what would you do?
4 make one big change to your job, what would it be?
5 spend €20,000 on improving your workplace, what changes would you make?

■ More information:
Grammar overview
page 103
▶ More practice:
Workbook page 50

should/shouldn't

People **shouldn't** *put their bags on the seat next to them. They* **should** *put them on the floor.*

You can use *should* and *shouldn't (should not)* to talk about people's proper behaviour. It's not as strong as *must*.

If we leave at 12 we **should** *be there by 2.*

You can also use *should* to talk about things that will probably happen.

You **should** *take a bottle of wine and some flowers when people invite you to dinner.*

You can also use *should* to give advice.

Compare with:
You **needn't tip** *the taxi driver = You* **don't have to tip** *taxi drivers.*

You can use *needn't* and *don't have* to to talk about things which are not obligatory.

A **Tell someone who is going to move to your country how to behave.**

1 Should I learn the language, or does everyone speak English?
You should learn the language. Not everyone can speak English.

2 When I get to the office in the morning, should I shake hands with everyone?

3 Should I invite colleagues out to lunch?

4 When I'm invited to a colleague's house, what should I take?

5 When I arrive at their house, what should I say in your language?

6 Is it OK to talk about politics and religion?

7 What should I say when I leave?

8 Should I phone to thank the person the next day? Or perhaps should I send them flowers?

■ More information:
Grammar overview
page 102
▶ More practice:
Workbook page 51

verbs with prepositions and particles

We **looked round** *the house and decided we wanted to buy it.*
Unemployment is **going up***.*

The prepositions and particles that follow verbs help to clarify or intensify their meaning.
The meeting **went through** *the minutes.*

Verbs followed by prepositions and particles can take objects.
You're **breaking up** *– I can't hear you.*
She **ran up** *a large bill. (= She spent a lot and had a large bill to pay.)*

Sometimes the meaning of verbs with particles is less clear. These are phrasal verbs.

A **Match the two parts of the definitions.**

If you ...

1 get on (well) with people,   **a** you contact them a short time after they have contacted you.

2 get back to someone,   **b** you leave it.

3 get through to someone,   **c** you reach them on the phone.

4 get off a bus or train,   **d** you like them and they like you.

B **Complete each sentence with the correct forms of the verbs in the box.**

break down	break up	calm down	come down	~~hold up~~

1 I'm sorry I'm late — I was <u>held</u> <u>up</u> in a traffic jam.

2 The photocopier has _____ _____. Can someone call the technician?

3 You're _____ _____! I can't hear you.

4 Don't panic! _____ _____!

5 Our prices are _____ _____ all the time.

■ More information:
Grammar overview
page 104
▶ More practice:
Workbook page 51

MODULE

6

GOING GLOBAL

This module looks at some of the issues and trends affecting the world today – manufacturing in developing countries, the growth of tourism, and business and the environment.

21   Today's trends

Grammar	present continuous for trends
Vocabulary	linking words; graph language
On the line	showing that you understand; completing a graph
Writing	a graph description

> What are the most important changes happening in your organisation, your town and your country at the moment?

22   Made in Cambodia

Grammar	present perfect with *already* and *yet*
Vocabulary	brands and manufacturing
On the line	asking about progress

> When you buy food, clothes or electronic goods, do you look to see where they are made? Why / why not?

23   Tourists are everywhere

Grammar	verb patterns: *ask, tell*, etc.
Vocabulary	customer delight and dissatisfaction
On the line	dealing with unhappy customers

> Is there anywhere in the world that tourists have yet not 'discovered'? Where is your favourite place? Is there a lot of tourism there?

24   Eco-friendly business

Vocabulary	*raise, increase, decrease, lower;* the environment
On the line	ending calls
Writing	a memo about a company's environmental policies

> Is there a business that has no effects at all on the environment?

♻ Grammar review and development 21–24

present continuous for trends

present perfect with *already* and *yet*

verb patterns: *ask, tell*, etc.

Listening and speaking

A 🔘 **21·1** **Miranda Rees of Crystal Ball Consultants is making a presentation about future trends. Identify the three trends.**

1 <u>globalisation</u>   2 _____   3 _____

B **Listen again. Underline the expressions that you hear.**

| For example   For instance   As a result   As a consequence   This has important consequences |
| Due to   <u>The first trend</u>   The second trend   The final point   First(ly)   Second(ly)   Third(ly) |

C **Listen once more and complete the information.**

Trend 1: Globalisation due to:

- free movement of capital around the world for <u>investment</u>
- barriers to _____ coming down
- cheaper _____ of goods
- cheaper _____ and _____ costs.

As a result, production of goods and services can move easily around the world, for example, to China for _____, and to _____ for many services like _____ _____ and _____ _____.

Trend 2: _____ _____. For example, in 40 years,

- in _____, the average age will be _____
- in _____, it will be _____.

This has important consequences for companies: the products and services that they _____ and the way that they _____ them. _____ may be less directed to younger people and more to _____.

Trend 3: _____ _____.

_____ weather is becoming more frequent, for example, _____ _____ and _____ _____ summers.

Your turn **D** **Work in pairs. Give a summary of the talk. (Don't use the exact words.)**

Grammar **present continuous for trends**

*Barriers to trade **are coming** down.*
*Summers **are getting** extremely hot.*

A **Complete the rule.**

You can use the present continuous to talk about trends happening _____.

B Change these sentences about current trends from the present simple to the present continuous.

1 People live longer, healthier lives.
People are living longer, healthier lives.

2 Company employees work longer hours each day.

3 Unemployment falls.

4 More and more young people go to university.

5 House prices rise very fast in some countries.

6 Traffic in cities moves more and more slowly.

C Work in pairs. Discuss the trends.

Is it true or false that people are ...

1 getting richer, but they aren't getting happier.

2 working longer hours than 10 years ago, but would prefer not to.

3 experiencing more stress than before.

■ More information:
Grammar review
and development
page 74
Grammar overview
page 98

▶ More practice:
Workbook page 53

D Talk about five important trends in your organisation or job.

My job is getting more and more difficult because ...

⏺N THE LINE **A** 🔊 **21.2** Naomi and Michael are journalists. Naomi has faxed Michael a graph, but he can't read it very well. Underline the expressions that you hear.

| I see. I understand. OK, I'm with you. |
| <u>I follow you.</u> That's it. That's correct. |
| I get it. Right. |

B Listen again. Which of these expressions do you hear? Write down the exact phrase that contains each expression.

rise
go up *it has gone up*
increase

level off

stay the same

go down
come down
decrease
fall

Your turn ▷ **C** Listen again. Complete the labels, figures and lines on the graph.

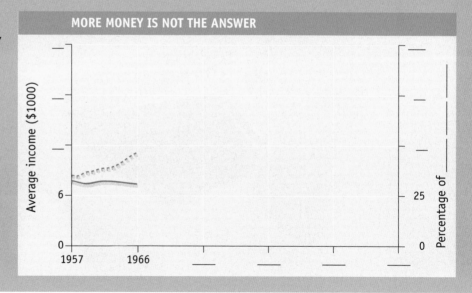

MORE MONEY IS NOT THE ANSWER

Writing **A** Write a description of the graph in your own words.

The graph compares income in the US since 1957 with percentages of people who say they are very happy.
In 1957, average income was about $9000, and about 30 per cent of people said they were very happy. ...

Checklist ✓ present continuous for trends: *People are getting richer, but they aren't getting happier.*

✓ linking words: *Firstly, As a consequence ...*

✓ show understanding: *I'm with you.*

22 Made in Cambodia

A Read the article.

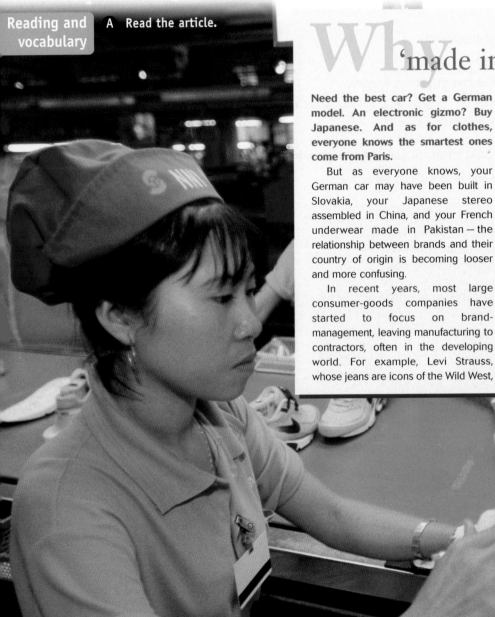

Why 'made in...' still matters

Need the best car? Get a German model. An electronic gizmo? Buy Japanese. And as for clothes, everyone knows the smartest ones come from Paris.

But as everyone knows, your German car may have been built in Slovakia, your Japanese stereo assembled in China, and your French underwear made in Pakistan — the relationship between brands and their country of origin is becoming looser and more confusing.

In recent years, most large consumer-goods companies have started to focus on brand-management, leaving manufacturing to contractors, often in the developing world. For example, Levi Strauss, whose jeans are icons of the Wild West, has just closed its last Texan plant in favour of contract manufacturing overseas.

Royal Doulton, a 200-year-old British pottery brand with a strong history, now manufactures in Indonesia and Bangladesh, while local rival Waterford Wedgwood prefers China. In effect, consumers have switched their loyalty from country to company.

So are we now blind to country of origin? Not quite, it seems. National stereotypes are far weaker than they were, but they are still alive. The Japanese are hard-working, the French glamorous, the British polite. For many classes of products, national or regional identity is always going to be important. Chinese toys are one thing — Chinese pasta sauce another completely.

B Match the expressions from the article to their meanings (a–f).

1 contractors
2 country of origin
3 developing world
4 manufacturing
5 plant
6 stereotype

a making goods
b a fixed idea about something that may or may not be true
c companies that make or do things for other companies
d another name for 'factory'
e the place where something is made
f all the countries that are poorer than those in the developed world

ON THE LINE **A** 22.1 **Martha Sanders works for Luther George (LG) Jeans. She is in Cambodia to talk to clothing contractors about manufacturing LG Jeans there. Her colleague Larry Winter, in New York, phones her to discuss progress. In which order do you hear these expressions?**

a How long have you been there now? __

b How's the trip going? |

c I think we can reach a deal with them. __

d I'll let you know how things go. __

e Keep me posted! __

f We haven't talked about price yet. __

g We've made good progress in the discussions so far. __

Your turn **B** **Student A looks at this page. Student B turns to page 157.**

Student A You work for a clothing company. Your colleague (Student B) is on a business trip to Manila in the Philippines to find a clothing contractor there. You phone them. Use some of the expressions from exercise A to check progress.

Grammar

present perfect with *already* and *yet*

A **Complete the rules.**

We've **already** discussed quantities, ...

You use *already* with the present perfect to say that something has happened.

... but we haven't agreed the price **yet**.

You use the present perfect (negative) with *yet* to say that something has _____ _____.

■ More information: Grammar review and development page 75 Grammar overview page 100
▶ More practice: Workbook page 55

B **Use the ideas below to talk about different stages in a business trip.**

1 pack my bags – phone for a taxi

I've already packed my bags, but I haven't phoned for a taxi yet.

2 arrive at the airport – get on the plane

3 land in Phnom Penh – pick up my baggage

4 get to the hotel – have dinner

5 see four contractors – choose one

6 decide the price – sign the contract

Listening

A 22.2 **Amity Jensen is an expert in the clothing industry. Listen to the interview with her. Which of the words from Reading and vocabulary exercise B do you hear?**

manufacturing, ...

B **Listen again. Write *T* (true) or *F* (false) according to Amity Jensen.**

1 Wages are typically $50 per month in Cambodia, $60 in Indonesia, $90 in the Philippines. T

2 Living costs in these places are lower than in Europe or America. __

3 Consumers in the developed world are interested in working conditions in contractors' plants. __

4 Conditions are better in the local factories that are *not* producing goods for the big brands. __

5 40 years ago Hong Kong was already rich. __

6 Now many of the clothing manufacturers in Hong Kong have become clothing retailers, with their own designers and their own brands. __

7 Hong Kong is not important in the global clothing industry. __

8 All low-cost manufacturing countries will stay like that forever. __

Your turn **C** **Work in pairs. Student A asks questions relating to the true answers in exercise B, and Student B answers them. (You do not have to use the exact words from the interview.)**

A: *How much do people in plants in Cambodia earn?*

B: *The wages there are typically $50 per month.*

Checklist

✓ manufacturing and brands: contractors, plant ...

✓ present perfect with *already* and *yet*: We've decided the price but we haven't signed the contract yet.

✓ ask about progress: How's the trip going?

23 Tourists are everywhere

A Look at this website.

ASAFLA travel

Do you want to see the real **Asia**, **Africa**, and **Latin America**? Meet local people and make a real contribution to the places that you travel through? We buy all our supplies locally, and use locally-owned accommodation.
Ready for a challenge? Try exploring the **Amazon**, rafting down the **Zambezi**, hiking in the **Andes** or trekking up **Mt. Kilimanjaro**.

Done   Internet

B Now answer the questions.

1 Do you like this sort of travel, or do you prefer to go to a hotel and lie on the beach?
2 Which button would you click on: Amazon, Zambezi, the Andes or Mt. Kilimanjaro?
3 For which age range of people are these holidays most suitable?

C Work in pairs. Answer the questions.

	Questionnaire
1 You are expected to help get the truck out of deep mud or sand when necessary. Are you prepared to do this, or would you just sit and wait for someone else to do it?	
2 You will travel with people who might want to play music till late into the night around the campfire. Would this drive you mad?	
3 You are expected to work hard and participate in all aspects of the trip, including putting up the tents and cooking. Would you enjoy this?	
4 We travel through areas that are very remote, often with no communication with the outside world. Would this be a shock for you?	

D Talk about your answers and those of your partner.

... says she could cope with tough conditions, but I prefer luxury hotels!

Vocabulary **A** Complete the commentary with the expressions in the box.

complaints
~~satisfied~~
delighted
word-of-mouth
dissatisfied
disappointed

> It's important to explain to customers what they can expect from your product or service. Hopefully they will be [1] satisfied and even [2]_____. But sometimes customers are [3]_____ and [4]_____. They don't get what they were expecting and they complain. It's important not to ignore [5]_____ – one unhappy customer will tell up to 10 other people about their bad experiences – this is a form of [6]_____ advertising that you do not want!

Grammar **verb patterns: *ask, tell,* etc.**

*He **told us to** get out and push.*
*They **told me not to** complain about the food.*

A Look at these
verb patterns.

advise ask tell expect want	someone	to do	something

advise ask tell	someone	not	to do	something

■ More information:
Grammar review
and development
page 75
Grammar overview
page 103
▶ More practice:
Workbook page 56

B An angry Asafla Travel customer is talking. Write what the tour leader told the group to do using the correct forms of the verbs in brackets.

1 put up the tents (ask)   *He asked us to put up the tents.*
2 clean the truck (tell)   **4** complain about the climate (tell/not)
3 drive all night (want)   **5** speak to the customer relations manager (advise)

ON THE LINE **A** **23.1** John Jones has been on a trip with Asafla Travel. Listen to the two conversations and answer the questions.

1 Which call is handled better by Asafla Travel? _____
2 Which of the problems in exercise B above does John Jones mention? ___|___

Your **turn** **B** Work in pairs. Student A looks at this page. Student B turns to page 158.

Student A You are the customer relations manager for Asafla Travel. One of your customers (Student B) phones to complain about the conditions on a trip that they went on. Use some of the expressions from exercise B to deal with the complaint politely. Discuss suitable compensation, for example:
● refund some of the cost of the holiday? If so, how much?
● discount off a future holiday?
(In some cases, you don't think the customer should get any compensation!)

Checklist ✓ verb patterns: ✓ vocabulary: ✓ deal with angry customers:
He told me not to complain.   *delighted, dissatisfied ...*   *What exactly was the problem?*

71

24 Eco-friendly business

Listening and vocabulary

A **24.1** *Boston World* is a newspaper in the north-east of the United States. Many of its articles are about environmental issues, and it has environment-friendly policies for its own operations. Listen to Katherine Green, its editor-in-chief, talking about these policies and complete the missing information.

BOSTON WORLD

1 For the newspaper, use paper that is __100__ per cent recycled.

2 Reduce _____ and _____ consumption in the offices.

3 Encourage staff to re-use paper and print on _____ _____.

4 Buy and use _____ printer ink cartridges.

5 Encourage staff to travel to work by public _____.

6 When executives and journalists travel, encourage them to go by _____.

7 Where they travel by plane, plant _____ to take up the carbon dioxide emissions that this causes.

Speaking

A Student A looks at this page. Students B and C turn to page 159 and Student D to page 159.

Student A
You are Katherine Green, Boston World's editor-in-chief. You have called a meeting with three department heads – the printing manager (Student B), the office manager (Student C) and the travel administrator (Student D). You want to know how much progress has been made in these areas.
What percentage of recycled paper did we use last year?
What percentage of recycled paper have we used this year?

	Last year	This year
Percentage of recycled paper used	80 per cent	84 per cent
Cost of electricity in printing plant		
Cost of electricity in office		
No. of employees cycling to work		
Travel: number of miles flown		
Number of trees planted		

B After the discussion, summarise the figures to the other members of the group.

Last year 80 per cent of the paper we used was recycled. This year ...

Vocabulary

*We have **reduced** the amount of electricity that we use.*

*We have **raised** the percentage of recycled paper that we use.*

These verbs are transitive – they take an object.

increase	decrease
raise	reduce
	lower

A **Use these verbs to talk about the figures in the table in Speaking exercise B.**

We have increased the amount of recycled paper that we use.

ON THE LINE **A** 24.2 **The public relations officer (PRO) for *Boston World* is answering queries on the phone. Look at the ways of ending calls. Match each ending to one of the three calls you hear.**

a __3__

A: Sounds good, can I get back to you about that? I'm sorry, I have to go now. I have an urgent call on another line.

B: No problem. I'll be hearing from you then.

A: Yes, I'll be in touch soon.

B: Bye.

A: Bye.

b ____

A: Sorry, but I have to rush. I have a meeting to go to.

B: OK. Thanks for confirming those figures.

A: It's a pleasure.

B: Bye.

A: Bye.

c ____

A: Look, I'm sorry, I have to go.

B: No problem. Thanks for clearing up that misunderstanding.

A: Sure. Don't hesitate to get back to me if you have any more questions.

B: OK. I'll do that. Bye.

A: Bye.

Your turn **B** **Work in pairs. Student A looks at this page. Student B turns to page 159.**

Student A

You are the public relations director for Boston World. You get three calls from different callers (Student B). Use this information to deal with them. You are in a hurry. Follow the instructions for each call.

- Conversation 1: The average number of people cycling to work each day is 34. There are 50 bike rack spaces in all.
- Conversation 2: Confirm the caller's figures.
- Conversation 3: Agree to the caller's suggestion for lunch.
- Then use an expression from exercise A above to end each call suitably.

Writing **A** **You are the PR officer for *Boston World*. Complete the memo to your boss, Katherine Green, about the calls that you get and the issues that people ask you about. (Imagine the questions that people ask and the information that you give.)**

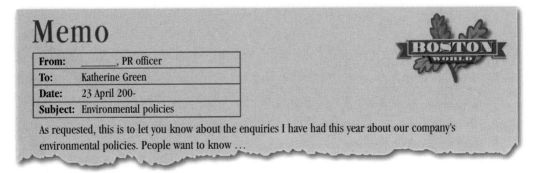

Memo

From:	_____, PR officer
To:	Katherine Green
Date:	23 April 200-
Subject:	Environmental policies

As requested, this is to let you know about the enquiries I have had this year about our company's environmental policies. People want to know …

Checklist ✓ the environment: *emissions, recycled …*   ✓ verbs: *raise, increase, reduce, decrease …*   ✓ end calls: *I have to go. / I'll be in touch.*

present continuous for trends

Affirmative	Negative	Questions
The country is getting rich.	The country isn't getting rich.	Is the country getting rich?

Transport of goods is getting cheaper.
You can use the present continuous to talk about trends happening now.

A A journalist takes these notes on a visit to China. Make complete sentences using the present continuous.

1 Economic growth 7 per cent per year – *The economy is growing at 7 per cent per year.*

2 Construction companies build a lot of new offices and apartments.

3 A lot of people leave the country and move to cities.

4 People earn more and more money.

5 Investors put a lot of money into China.

6 Foreign companies open new shops.

B Ask and answer questions about trends in Nordland using the present continuous.

	10 years ago	5 years ago	This year
1 Population	35 million	33 million	29 million
2 Average age	45	48	49
3 Unemployment	0.8 million	1.1 million	1.9 million
4 New companies	10,000	6,500	3,300
5 Average salary	€30,000	€28,000	€26,000
6 Confidence in the future (10 years ago = 100)	100	87	79

1 population grow/fall?
   A: *Is the population growing or falling?*
   B: *It's falling.*
2 average age increase/decrease?
3 unemployment rise/fall?
4 number of new companies go up/down?
5 people get richer/poorer?
6 people feel more confident / less confident?

Note that you don't use some verbs in the present continuous
in their main meaning

belong to	consist of	contain	exist
have	include	involve	lack
owe	prefer	seem	want

C Correct the statements about the European Union (EU) where necessary. Write a tick when they are correct.

1 Twenty-five countries are belonging to the EU.
   Twenty-five countries belong to the EU.
2 The new members include Poland, the Czech Republic and eight other countries. ✔
3 The Scandinavian members are consisting of Denmark, Sweden and Finland.
4 Economic growth in different countries seems to depend on a combination of factors.
5 Ireland owes its success largely to its membership of the EU.
6 Countries are preferring to use English in discussions, rather than French.
7 Some people in the UK are wanting to leave the EU.

■ More information: Grammar overview page 98

present perfect with *already* and *yet*

Affirmative	Negative	Questions
We've already talked.	We haven't talked yet.	Have we talked yet?

*We've **already** finished the designs, ...*

You use *already* with the present perfect to say that something has happened.

*..., but we haven't started production **yet**.*

You use the present perfect (negative) with *yet* to say that something has not happened.

A Work in pairs. An electronics company is building a new plant. Every three months, someone asks about progress. Ask and answer questions.

 1 prepare the site / start building
   A: *Have you prepared the site?*
   B: *We've already prepared the site, but we haven't started building yet.*

 2 build walls / put on roof

 3 connect electricity / install machines

 4 install machines / start manufacturing

 5 start manufacturing / launch the product

 6 launch the product / sell any

B A boss tells her personal assistant to do things, but the PA is extremely efficient and has already done everything. Give the PA's answers as in the example.

 1 I'd go and see Bob about the product launch.   *I've already seen him.*

 2 Please, could you write a letter to Temco?

 3 Now, can you send a fax to GLX?

 4 It's time to phone Williamson's.

 5 Then you can get the latest figures from the sales department.

 6 You can go and have lunch now.

■ More information: Grammar overview page 100

▶ More practice: Workbook page 61

Verb patterns: *ask, tell,* etc.

A The PA in exercise B above is having tea with a colleague. She explains to her colleague what her boss told her to do that morning. Rewrite sentences using the verbs in the box as in the example.

advise   ask   tell   expect   want

 1 *She advised me to go and see Bob about the product launch.*

B Now imagine the PA's boss told her *not* to do certain things. Make negative sentences, as in the example.

 1 talk to anyone else (ask)   *She asked me not to talk to anyone else.*

 2 post it (tell)

 3 phone them (tell)

 4 waste time (advise)

 5 give the figures to other departments (ask)

■ More information: Grammar overview page 103

MODULE

7

WRITING RESOURCE

This module gives further practice in writing letters, faxes, e-mails and other short texts.

25   A delayed project

a company memo

an informal e-mail exchange

> Why do things usually take longer than we think they will? What are some typical causes of stress at work?

26   Consumer complaints

a letter of complaint

a reply to a letter of complaint

a company memo

> What are some typical causes of complaints to companies? How should companies react to complaints?

27   A new opening

sending, accepting and declining invitations

> Does your organisation (school, company, etc.) have any events to which it invites people? If so, what are they?

28   Finding an agent

a fax exchange

> Do you send faxes, or do you only use e-mail? When are faxes useful?

29   Remote working

a company memo

an e-mail exchange

> Some organisations have one 'no e-mail day' every week. Would this be possible in your organisation?

30   A world trip

a text message

an informal e-mail

a postcard

> When you're on holiday, do you send text messages to your friends instead of postcards? Why / why not?

   Review and development 25–30

25 A delayed project

Memo **A** Look at this schedule for a building project.

STAGES	J	F	M	A	M	J	J	A	S	O	N	D	J
1 Complete walls	×	×											
2 Put on roof		×	×	×	×								
3 Install doors and windows				×	×	×							
4 Install electricity and computer network					×	×	×	×					
5 Paint inside of building							×	×	×				
6 Install furniture								×		×	×		
7 Move in										×			?

× = planned; × = actual

1 to 3 – very cold weather
4 – technical problems
5 – strike by painters' union
6 – wrong furniture ordered: it had to be sent back to suppliers.

B Now complete the memo using the information in the schedule. Give reasons for the delays.

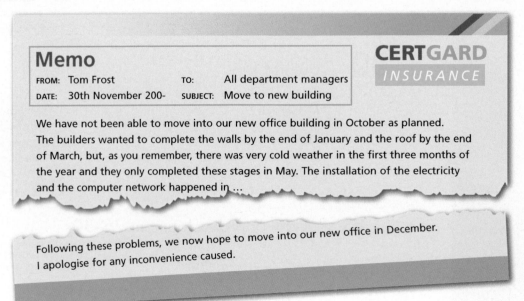

Memo

CERTGARD INSURANCE

FROM: Tom Frost TO: All department managers
DATE: 30th November 200- SUBJECT: Move to new building

We have not been able to move into our new office building in October as planned.
The builders wanted to complete the walls by the end of January and the roof by the end
of March, but, as you remember, there was very cold weather in the first three months of
the year and they only completed these stages in May. The installation of the electricity
and the computer network happened in …

Following these problems, we now hope to move into our new office in December.
I apologise for any inconvenience caused.

E-mail exchange

A **Look at the ways to begin and end an e-mail.**

> **Openings**
>
> If you don't know the person very well, you can start as in a letter.
> *Dear Mr ...,* or *Dear Ms ...,*
>
> If you know them better, you can start with their first name.
> *Dear Ray / Dear Jane,*
>
> If you know them even better, you can write *Hello* or *Hi.*
> *Hi, Ray,*
>
> | **Endings** | More formal | | | | | Less formal |
> |---|---|---|---|---|---|---|
> | | *Regards,* | *Best regards,* | *All best wishes,* | *Best wishes,* | *All the best,* | *Best,* |

B **Read this e-mail from Tom Frost to a friend.**

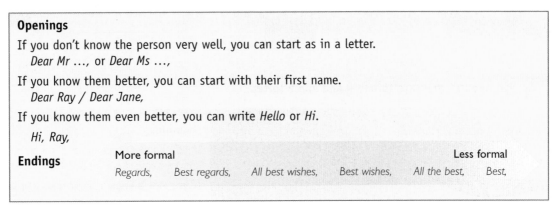

Hi, Ray,

Thanks again for lunch last week. You remember I told you about the delayed move to our new office building? Well, there's another delay! My boss and all the other managers are going crazy – they're blaming me, when they should blame the builders and all the other people responsible.

I feel so stressed! I can't sleep at night and I can't concentrate on my work during the day. You said you know a good stress counsellor. Please can you send me her details?

All the best,

Tom

C **You are Ray Lindsay. Write a reply to Tom Frost.**

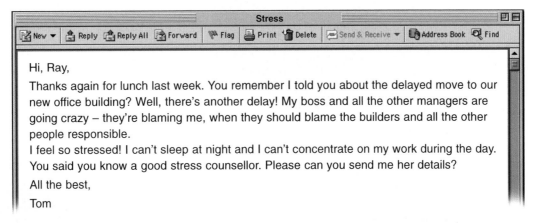

Hi, Tom,

I'm sorry to hear about the delayed move. I can understand why you're feeling so stressed!

[Give some advice] You could .... *[Give some more advice]* Why not ...

[Give Tom the name and e-mail address of the stress counsellor – Sarah Connell: s.connell@libserve.com] The name of the ...

[Say you are attaching an article about her from Business Month magazine] Please find attached ...

[Say you hope that he likes the article] I hope ...

Good luck!

All the best,

D **Now write Tom's reply to Ray.**

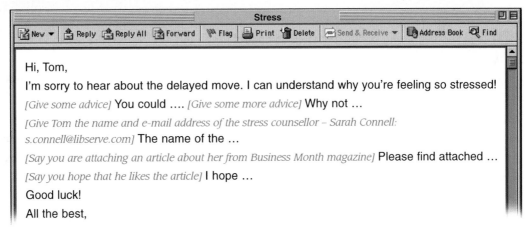

Ray hi,

Sorry not to get back to you earlier. I contacted Sarah Connell and I had my first session with her on Friday. She's very good - I'm already feeling better!

[Say you couldn't open the attachment with the article about Sarah Connell. Ask Ray to send it again.] Unfortunately I couldn't ... Would it be possible ...

[Say you will be in touch again soon.] I'll be ...

All the best,

Tom

26 Consumer complaints

Letter **A** Look at the ways to begin and end a letter.

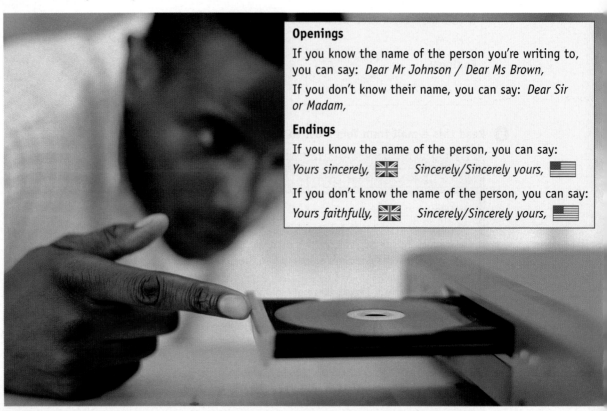

Openings

If you know the name of the person you're writing to, you can say: *Dear Mr Johnson / Dear Ms Brown,*

If you don't know their name, you can say: *Dear Sir or Madam,*

Endings

If you know the name of the person, you can say:

Yours sincerely, 🇬🇧   *Sincerely/Sincerely yours,* 🇺🇸

If you don't know the name of the person, you can say:

Yours faithfully, 🇬🇧   *Sincerely/Sincerely yours,* 🇺🇸

B Read the beginning of this letter of complaint. Then put the rest of the letter in the correct order.

348 Henbury Hill
Bristol BS49 2YU
Tel 0117 892 3411

Gizmo Electronics
Attn. Customer Experience Manager
Forsoken Industrial Estate
Croydon CR45 2EG
31st March 200–

Re: Defective CD player

Dear Sir or Madam,
I have had a series of problems with

a ☐ to the wrong address. When I finally got it, the CDs 'jumped' when I tried to play them. I sent

b ☐ Yours faithfully,
Brian Johnson

c ☐ the CD player that I bought last November. I spoke to someone at your call centre and they told me to write to you. First it was delivered

d ☐ the machine back for repair, and you kept it for two months. I got it back yesterday, but the machine still does not work properly. I'm writing now

e ☐ to ask for a complete refund, plus an extra amount to cover the inconvenience that I have experienced.

f ☐ Looking forward to hearing from you,

C Choose one of the following gadgets. Write a letter to the supplier to complain that it does not work properly and to ask for a replacement. (Invent the make and model.)

- a washing machine that stops in the middle of the cycle for no reason.
- an oven that doesn't heat up to the right temperature.
- a toaster that burns toast after only a few seconds.

Reply

A Complete the reply to the letter in exercise B with the words a–e.

   a replacement   **b** packaging   **c** guarantee   **d** invoice   **e** refund

Gizmo
Electronics

Forsoken Industrial Estate
Croydon CR45 2EG
Tel/fax 020 9872 8333
www.gizmo-electronics.com

Mr Brian Johnson
348 Henbury Hill
Bristol BS49 2YU

10th April 200-

Re: Defective CD player

Dear Mr Johnson,

Thank you for you letter of 31st March detailing the problems that you have experienced with your CD player. Unfortunately, we cannot consider your request for a ^{1}_____: under the terms of the ^{2}_____, we can only offer you a ^{3}_____ machine.

Please return your CD player in its original ^{4}_____, along with a copy of the ^{5}_____, and we will send you a new machine to replace it.

Yours sincerely,

James Stevens

Customer Experience Manager

Memo

A Read this company memo.

From: James Stevens, Customer Experience Manager
To: All call centre staff
Date: 12th April 200-

Gizmo
Electronics

Re: Anderson 400 CD players

Over the past three months I have received a lot of complaints from customers about problems with the Anderson 400 CD player. I have been in touch with the manufacturers, and they know about the problem. They are replacing all the defective machines at no cost to us.
If you have calls from customers about this model of CD player, just tell them to return the machine and we will replace it free of charge.
Please do everything you can to stop customers writing to me about this model – I have spent too much time on this recently.

B Think of something that might cause a lot of wasted time in your company, school or organisation.

For example:

- unreliable products sold by your company but made by another company.
- people who phone one number when they should phone another number.
- people who phone to ask about products or services that the organisation does not provide.

Write an internal memo.

Say:

- what the problem is.
- how it can be solved.

27 A new opening

Invitations

A Jennifer Powell, the human resources director for Global Credit Bank in Singapore, visits different health clubs to talk about membership for her employees (unit 9). Read the invitation that she receives from Elan Health Clubs.

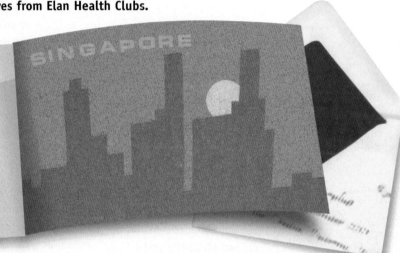

Elan Health Clubs Singapore
request the pleasure of the company of

Jennifer Powell

at the opening of their new health club
800 North Bridge Road, Singapore 179099
Friday 2nd April at 6.00 pm
Please reply by e-mail to erica.fox@elan.sg

B Now read the letter that came with the invitation. In each of the lines 1–10 there is one wrong word. Cross out the wrong word and write the correct word in the space at the end of the line.

elan
HEALTH CLUBS
SINGAPORE

Global Credit Bank, Singapore
Attn: Jennifer Powell, Human Resources Director
934 North Bridge Road
Singapore 179098

15th March 200-

55 HARPER ROAD
SINGAPORE 369677
TEL +9382 2310,
FAX +9382 2312

Dear Ms Powell,

1 Thank you for coming to visit our facilities last week. I hope you ~~find~~ your visit   found
2 useful. I have some very good new! I wasn't able to talk about this last week as the   _____
3 plans were still confident, but we have now finalised details of a new health club   _____
4 that will open next month in the same block of your bank! I don't know if you   _____
5 have made your decide about the health club that your company will use,   _____
6 but the location of the new health new club will be ideal for your employs.   _____
7 We are having the open of the health club on 2nd April at 6.30pm – please   _____
8 see the attach invitation.   _____
9 I hope you will be able to come to see the new club for your. Please could   _____
6 you allow me know if you will be able to attend?   _____
10 Many thanks.   _____

Looking forward to hearing from you,

Best wishes,

Erica Fox

Erica Fox, Manager, Elan Health Clubs

C Read Jennifer Powell's reply to Erica Fox's invitation and letter. In most of the lines 1–7 there is one word that does not fit. Write the word in the space at the end of the line. If a line is correct, put a tick (✔) in the space.

1 Thank you for a very useful meeting last week. I enjoyed visiting your facilities very much –   ✔

2 I was very to impressed.   to

3 Thank you for of the invitation to the opening of your new health club. Unfortunately, I will   _____

4 be on holiday that week. Please can you send an invitation to my assistant, Samuel Tang –   _____

5 I am sure he will want to attend. We haven't made a decision about the club we are at going   _____

6 to use. Samuel will give me a full report about your new facilities, no doubt! We will be in   _____

7 the touch later about our decision after we have discussed things further.   _____

Best regards,

Jennifer Powell, HRD, Global Credit Bank, Singapore

D Read about these invitations that you have received, all for the same evening.

- a seminar about latest developments in your profession or industry.
- an open evening at a supplier's with a guided tour of their new manufacturing plant.
- a talk by a business expert about how to increase employees' motivation and productivity.
- the opening of an exhibition of paintings by your favourite artist. (Your boss has asked you to buy some paintings for your office building and you think this artist might be a good choice.)

E Write an e-mail to the organisers of the event you want to go to, thanking them and accepting the invitation.

Thank you for the invitation to your event on 15th April. This is to confirm that ...

[Ask if you can bring a colleague.]   Would it be possible to ...

[Give the name of your colleague.]

[Ask for directions on how to get to the event.]

[Ask what time the event ends.]

F Now write an e-mail to the organisers of another of the events in D, explaining that no one from your organisation can attend, but asking the organisers to inform you of similar events in the future.

Thank you for your invitation to ...

Unfortunately ...

I'd be grateful if ...

28 Finding an agent

A Clara Rios has developed an energy drink and is now looking for agents to sell it in different countries. Read the fax that she writes to a possible agent in Japan.

FAX

Clara Rios SA

Date: 14th August 200-	Rua Mamore 905
Fax no.: +81 42 926 1341	Sao Paulo, Brazil
No. of pages inc. this one: 1	Tel +55 25 39 1598,
	Fax +55 25 39 1599

From:	Clara Rios
To:	All-Nippon Food Imports, Tokyo
Attn:	Mr Masahiko Kato

Re: Import agents for Amajuice

Dear Mr Kato,

The Japanese Consulate here in Sao Paulo gave me your name. I have developed an energy drink called Amajuice, with secret ingredients from the Amazon jungle. I am looking for an agent to import and distribute the drink in Japan. I am visiting various countries in Asia next month, and I hope to be in Tokyo the week of 10th September. If you would like to meet to discuss the possibilities, please let me know.

I look forward to hearing from you.

Best regards,

Clara Rios

Clara Rios (Ms)

B This is the reply. Put the words in each line in the correct order.

Date: 16th August 200-	**From:** Masahiko Kato
Fax no.: +55 25 39 1599	**To:** Clara Rios SA, Sao Paulo
No. of pages inc. this one: 1	**Attn:** Clara Rios

Re: Import agents for Amajuice

Rios Ms Dear,

thanks Many for fax your

are We one biggest of the importers food Japan into of

drink sounds Your interesting very energy

would I like much very meet to you when come Japan you to month next

about How coming to office my Tuesday on 11th 3 pm at?

look I forward discussing to you with the possibilities

could Please confirm you that date this suitable is?

regards Best

Masahiko Kato

C Read the fax Masahiko Kato sent after the meeting. In each of the lines 1–8 there is one wrong word. Cross out the wrong word and write the correct word in the space at the end of the line.

FAX

All-Nippon Food Imports
9-8-1 Atago, Minato-ku, Tokyo
Tel 81 42 926 1340, Fax 81 42 926 1341

Date: 17th September 200-	**From:** Masahiko Kato
Fax no.: +55 25 39 1599	**To:** Clara Rios SA, Sao Paulo
No. of pages inc. this one: 1	**Attn:** Clara Rios

Re: Agency agreement

Dear Ms Rios,

1 Thank you very much for ~~come~~ to see me in Tokyo last week and for the very   coming

2 interesting discuss that we had. This is to summarise what we agreed. For three   _____

3 years, starting on January 1st last year, we will import 500,000 cans of Amajuice a   _____

4 year for sale in Japan at a retail prize of about US$1.50. We will pay you 85 US cents   _____

5 per can. Shipping costs and import tax are to be paying by your organisation.   _____

6 We will re-negotiate this agreement after three years. We talked on the possibility   _____

7 of manufacturing Amajuice under licence in Japan if the sell quantities justify this.   _____

8 This will of course be subject to a new agree. But we will cross this bridge when   _____
we come to it!

I'm sending you our standard agreement by DHL courier today. Please sign and
return it as soon as possible.

Best regards,

Masahiko Kato

D Complete Clara Rios's reply. Choose the correct alternative for each space.

Agency Agreement

Dear Mr Kato,

Thank you very much for your fax of 17th September, and the Agency Agreement, which arrived this morning. I have asked my lawyers to check the agreement and will ¹ _b_ it next week.

Meanwhile, I will ² ____ the arrangements for transport of the ³ ____ of Amajuice to Tokyo, starting in January next year. We are looking at ⁴ ____ of 40,000 to 50,000 cans per month, depending on ⁵ ____ . We will probably ⁶ ____ the goods via Porto Alegre in southern Brazil, using our normal shipping agents. (They have been very ⁷ ____ in the past in shipping our goods to other export markets.) We will ⁸ ____ these arrangements in the ⁹ ____ months.

Best regards,

Clara Rios

1	**a** re-send	**b** return	**c** refund	**d** reply
2	**a** control	**b** convert	**c** check	**d** combine
3	**a** containment	**b** continents	**c** continuations	**d** consignments
4	**a** quantities	**b** masses	**c** groups	**d** bunches
5	**a** asking	**b** questions	**c** queries	**d** demand
6	**a** shape	**b** ship	**c** shop	**d** shout
7	**a** hopeful	**b** reliable	**c** likable	**d** notable
8	**a** consent	**b** content	**c** confirm	**d** conform
9	**a** coming	**b** came	**c** come	**d** comes

29 Remote working

A Complete this memo from the chief partner (owner) of a firm of architects. The missing words are related to the words in brackets.

From	Lucy Rogerson
To	All employees
Date	7th July 200-
Subject	Remote working

Rogerson & Partners

As you know, our offices here in ¹*central* (centre) London are extremely ² _____ (expense).

The main cost is rent — this has ³ _____ (double) in the past six years. We have considered moving to an out-of-town site, but it is ⁴ _____ (importance) for the partners to be near the government offices because, as you know, we do a lot of work with them.

We have therefore ⁵ _____ (decide) to move to a ⁶ _____ (small) office, where the partners and some employees will ⁷ _____ (continue) to work. However, other employees will work from home, meeting colleagues and clients at the office when necessary. We are therefore ⁸ _____ (look) for employees who are willing to work from home — we will, of course, provide all necessary ⁹ _____ (equip) and support.

Please let me know by next Monday if you are willing to work from home, or if you prefer to continue to work at the central office.

A An employee at Rogerson and Partners writes an e-mail to Lucy Rogerson. Look at the handwritten notes and complete the e-mail.

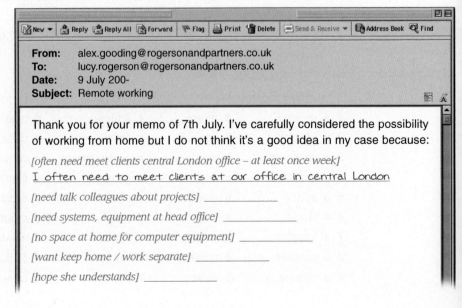

New ▼ | Reply | Reply All | Forward | Flag | Print | Delete | Send & Receive ▼ | Address Book | Find

From:	alex.gooding@rogersonandpartners.co.uk
To:	lucy.rogerson@rogersonandpartners.co.uk
Date:	9 July 200-
Subject:	Remote working

Thank you for your memo of 7th July. I've carefully considered the possibility of working from home but I do not think it's a good idea in my case because:

[often need meet clients central London office – at least once week]
I often need to meet clients at our office in central London

[need talk colleagues about projects] _____

[need systems, equipment at head office] _____

[no space at home for computer equipment] _____

[want keep home / work separate] _____

[hope she understands] _____

B Another employee at Rogerson and Partners writes an e-mail to Lucy Rogerson. Look at the handwritten notes and complete the e-mail.

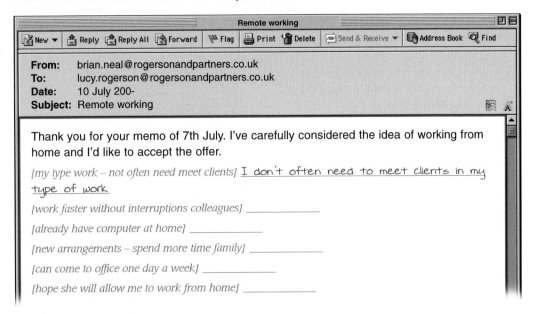

	Remote working	
New ▼	Reply	Reply All	Forward	Flag	Print	Delete	Send & Receive ▼	Address Book	Find

From: brian.neal@rogersonandpartners.co.uk
To: lucy.rogerson@rogersonandpartners.co.uk
Date: 10 July 200-
Subject: Remote working

Thank you for your memo of 7th July. I've carefully considered the idea of working from home and I'd like to accept the offer.

[my type work – not often need meet clients] I don't often need to meet clients in my type of work

[work faster without interruptions colleagues] _____

[already have computer at home] _____

[new arrangements – spend more time family] _____

[can come to office one day a week] _____

[hope she will allow me to work from home] _____

C Complete Lucy's reply to Alex's e-mail. Put the verbs in brackets in the correct form.

	Remote working	
New ▼	Reply	Reply All	Forward	Flag	Print	Delete	Send & Receive ▼	Address Book	Find

From: lucy.rogerson@rogersonandpartners.co.uk
To: alex.gooding@rogersonandpartners.co.uk
Date: 9 July 200-
Subject: RE: Remote working

Thanks for your reply to my memo, in which you say you wish to continue [1]working (work) at the office. You claim that you often need [2]_____ _____ (see) clients, but I [3]_____ _____ (look) at your job description and [4]_____ (speak) to Bob, your manager, and I [5]_____ (see) that in fact you have very little client contact. You say that you [6]_____ (need) to talk to colleagues about projects, but if you work from home, you can do this on the phone.

With regard to space at home for computer equipment, all you need is space on a table for a laptop computer – we [7]_____ _____ (provide) the laptop for you.

I [8]_____ _____ (decide) that you should work from home, starting on 1st August. Please see your manager re the laptop computer that we [9]_____ _____ (supply).

D Write Lucy's e-mail in reply to Brian's e-mail in exercise B. Include the following points:

- Thank Brian for his e-mail and for agreeing to work from home.
  Many thanks for your reply to my memo. Thank you for agreeing to work from home.
- Tell him that he will start working from home on 1st August.
- Say that as he already has a computer, he will receive a special payment of £1000. If he prefers not to use his own computer, he can get a laptop computer from the organisation.
- Ask him to discuss arrangements for homeworking with Caroline, his manager.
- End suitably.

30 A world trip

Text message

A Look at the ways to make messages shorter in mobile phone text messages (and personal e-mails).

- abbreviations
  GTG = got to go   WKND = weekend
- unusual spellings
  EVRY = every   GONNA = going to
- letters used for words
  B = be   OIC = Oh I see   Y = why
- numbers used for words or in words
  2 = to, too   B4 = before
  EVRY1 = everyone

B 'Translate' the exchange of text messages between Samantha and her friend Anna into ordinary English.

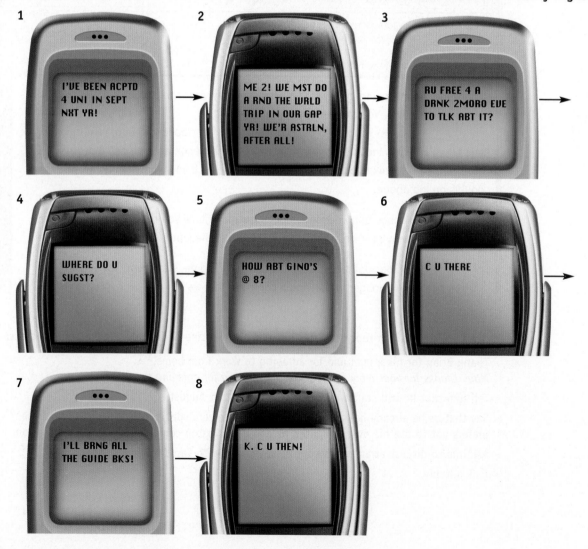

1
I'VE BEEN ACPTD 4 UNI IN SEPT NXT YR!

2
ME 2! WE MST DO A RND THE WRLD TRIP IN OUR GAP YR! WE'R ASTRLN, AFTER ALL!

3
RU FREE 4 A DRNK 2MORO EVE TO TLK ABT IT?

4
WHERE DO U SUGST?

5
HOW ABT GINO'S @ 8?

6
C U THERE

7
I'LL BRNG ALL THE GUIDE BKS!

8
K. C U THEN!

C Text a friend to make a suggestion. Write the exchange of text messages.

E-mail **A** You can use emoticons in personal e-mails and text messages. Match the emoticons to their meanings.

1	:-)	**a**	shouting
2	:-(	**b**	crying
3	:-D	**c**	happy
4	:-( )	**d**	I can't say anything
5	:'-(	**e**	having a cold
6	:-~)	**f**	laughing
7	:-X	**g**	sad
8	: @	**h**	shocked

B Read the e-mail that Samantha sends to a friend from an Internet café, while she is on her world trip. She uses some of the emoticons. Put them in the correct places.

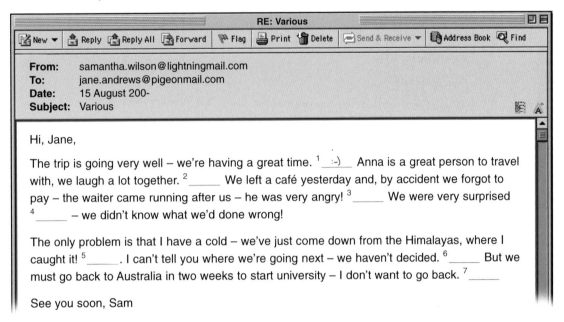

RE: Various

New ▾ | Reply | Reply All | Forward | Flag | Print | Delete | Send & Receive ▾ | Address Book | Find

From: samantha.wilson@lightningmail.com
To: jane.andrews@pigeonmail.com
Date: 15 August 200-
Subject: Various

Hi, Jane,

The trip is going very well – we're having a great time. ¹ __:-)__ Anna is a great person to travel with, we laugh a lot together. ² _____ We left a café yesterday and, by accident we forgot to pay – the waiter came running after us – he was very angry! ³ _____ We were very surprised ⁴ _____ – we didn't know what we'd done wrong!

The only problem is that I have a cold – we've just come down from the Himalayas, where I caught it! ⁵ _____ . I can't tell you where we're going next – we haven't decided. ⁶ _____ But we must go back to Australia in two weeks to start university – I don't want to go back. ⁷ _____

See you soon, Sam

Postcard **A** Read the postcard from Anna to a friend.

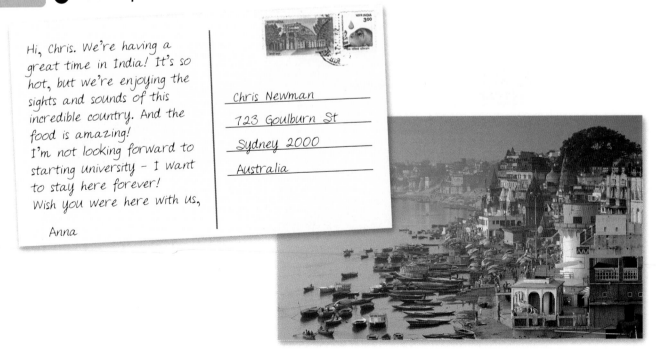

Hi, Chris. We're having a great time in India! It's so hot, but we're enjoying the sights and sounds of this incredible country. And the food is amazing!
I'm not looking forward to starting university – I want to stay here forever!
Wish you were here with us,

Anna

Chris Newman
123 Goulburn St
Sydney 2000
Australia

B You are on holiday. Write a postcard to a friend. Say that you don't want to go back home and give a reason.

A Certgard Insurance (unit 25) finally move into their new offices. But the builders have not completed the work properly. Write a letter to them from Tom Frost, at Certgard. Use the points below and end it suitably.

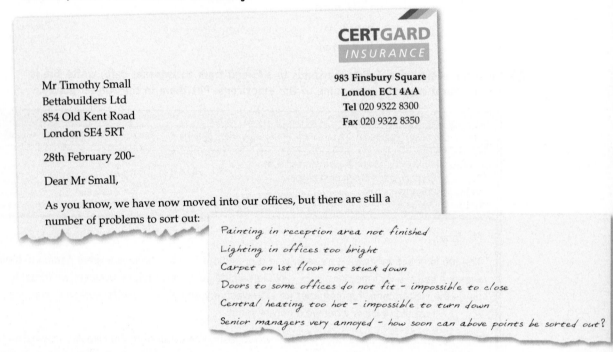

CERTGARD INSURANCE

983 Finsbury Square
London EC1 4AA
Tel 020 9322 8300
Fax 020 9322 8350

Mr Timothy Small
Bettabuilders Ltd
854 Old Kent Road
London SE4 5RT

28th February 200-

Dear Mr Small,

As you know, we have now moved into our offices, but there are still a number of problems to sort out:

Painting in reception area not finished
Lighting in offices too bright
Carpet on 1st floor not stuck down
Doors to some offices do not fit – impossible to close
Central heating too hot – impossible to turn down
Senior managers very annoyed – how soon can above points be sorted out?

B Write an e-mail from Tom Frost to his friend Ray Lindsay, using the following notes.

You have seen Sarah Connell (stress counsellor recommended by Ray) about 10 times – some improvement at first – but you have been under more stress recently because of problems with new building senior managers extremely angry – they blame you for not dealing with builders efficiently – you are thinking about moving to another company – does Ray know of any possibilities in his company?

C Complete this fax from Jennifer Powell to Erica Fox (unit 27). The missing words are related to the words in brackets.

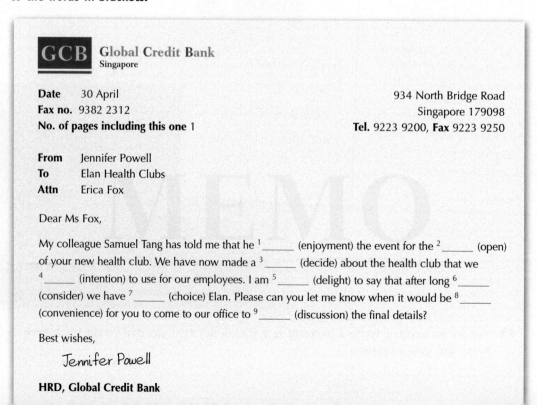

GCB Global Credit Bank
Singapore

Date 30 April
Fax no. 9382 2312
No. of pages including this one 1

934 North Bridge Road
Singapore 179098
Tel. 9223 9200, **Fax** 9223 9250

From Jennifer Powell
To Elan Health Clubs
Attn Erica Fox

Dear Ms Fox,

My colleague Samuel Tang has told me that he [1] _____ (enjoyment) the event for the [2] _____ (open) of your new health club. We have now made a [3] _____ (decide) about the health club that we [4] _____ (intention) to use for our employees. I am [5] _____ (delight) to say that after long [6] _____ (consider) we have [7] _____ (choice) Elan. Please can you let me know when it would be [8] _____ (convenience) for you to come to our office to [9] _____ (discussion) the final details?

Best wishes,

Jennifer Powell

HRD, Global Credit Bank

D Write a fax from Masahiko Kato to Clara Rios (unit 28). Base the fax on the points below and end it suitably.

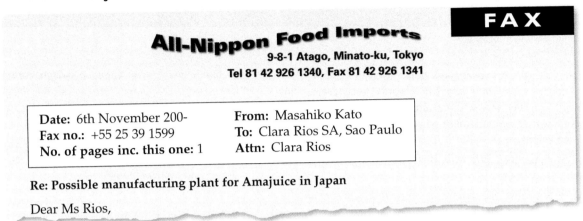

FAX

All-Nippon Food Imports
9-8-1 Atago, Minato-ku, Tokyo
Tel 81 42 926 1340, Fax 81 42 926 1341

Date: 6th November 200-
Fax no.: +55 25 39 1599
No. of pages inc. this one: 1

From: Masahiko Kato
To: Clara Rios SA, Sao Paulo
Attn: Clara Rios

Re: Possible manufacturing plant for Amajuice in Japan

Dear Ms Rios,

Amajuice – sales in Japan for 1st year very successful – 1 million cans – twice the objective

next year's objective – 3 million cans

now interested in manufacturing Amajuice in Japan – would like to discuss possibilities – site available for plant just outside Tokyo

possible come to Sao Paulo in the next two weeks to discuss plans? dates?

E Complete this e-mail from Brian, an architect at Rogerson and Partners (unit 29) who works from home, to Jill, an administrative assistant in the office. Use the correct forms of the verbs in brackets.

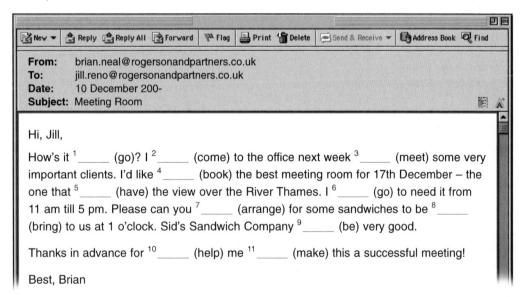

New ▾ | Reply | Reply All | Forward | Flag | Print | Delete | Send & Receive ▾ | Address Book | Find

From: brian.neal@rogersonandpartners.co.uk
To: jill.reno@rogersonandpartners.co.uk
Date: 10 December 200-
Subject: Meeting Room

Hi, Jill,

How's it ¹_____ (go)? I ²_____ (come) to the office next week ³_____ (meet) some very important clients. I'd like ⁴_____ (book) the best meeting room for 17th December – the one that ⁵_____ (have) the view over the River Thames. I ⁶_____ (go) to need it from 11 am till 5 pm. Please can you ⁷_____ (arrange) for some sandwiches to be ⁸_____ (bring) to us at 1 o'clock. Sid's Sandwich Company ⁹_____ (be) very good.

Thanks in advance for ¹⁰_____ (help) me ¹¹_____ (make) this a successful meeting!

Best, Brian

F Unlike her friend Samantha, Anna (unit 30) wants to return from India to start university. Write a postcard from Anna to a friend, including the expressions in the box. Begin and end the postcard suitably.

| Australian | comfortable | food | go back | hot | India |
| Nice | room | tiring | very | want | weather |

G Anna and Samantha have started university in Sydney. Translate the text message from Anna to Samantha into ordinary English.

IT'S GR8 2 B BACK, BUT I'M NSTLGC 4 INDIA. LETS GO TO INDN RESTRT THIS EVE. HOW ABT 8? HAVE U TRIED KHAN'S - IT'S V G. I'LL BRNG ALL THE PIX! C U!

Vocabulary builder

When you work on vocabulary, don't just think about individual words. Think about how words go together – how a word typically goes with certain other words. When you write down vocabulary, note down some of these typical combinations.

For example, don't just write down the word *company*, note down:

- combinations: *a design company, a furniture company, a leisure company, a not-for-profit company,*

a pharmaceuticals company, a venture capital company, the Swedish company Stora, the world's biggest car company, construction companies, large consumer-goods companies

- complete sentences: *Channel 7 is one of Europe's most exciting television companies. Avon gets its raw materials from specialist companies.*

Word combinations: *Have*

- Look at these 'ordinary' uses of *have* in *Best Practice Pre-intermediate*.
  Paris has some of the best public transport of any city.
  Tommy has a knee injury.
  Do you have enough time?
  I have your catalogue in front of me.
  You have a budget of $4 million.
  Northern Europe will have a more Mediterranean-type climate.
  I only have a very small garden.
  The plan may or may not have the effects we want.
  We've had problems with our e-mail.
  Future World only had two million visitors last year.

- *Have* is used to talk about experiences, journeys, etc.
  Have a great day out at Farwest!
  I hope you all had a pleasant trip back.

- *Have* is used to ask for things.
  Can I have a table for two?

- *Have* is often used with food and drink.

have	a glass/bottle of wine
	a coffee
	a sandwich
	breakfast
	lunch
	dinner

It'll be great to have this drink together.

Word combinations: *make* and *do*

Make

- *Make* is used to talk about actions with some nouns. These nouns all occur in this book, most with *make*.

make a/an		make a/an	
	announcement		enquiry
	arrangement		investment
	booking		list
	calculation		mistake
	change		note
	contribution	make	money
	decision		progress

Do you make a list of everything you have to do?
We don't often make mistakes in our recruitment.
We will make $5 million profit in the second year.
Text a friend in order to make a suggestion.
Make three calls to the public relations manager at Boston World.
If you'd like to make a booking, please press 1.
We haven't made any final decisions yet.
They made an announcement in Turkish.
We've made good progress in the discussions so far.

- These expressions are often used instead of verbs.
  You can make a real contribution. = You can really contribute something.
  What changes would you make? = What would you change?

- *Make* is also used to talk about producing things.
  The company makes high-tech products.
  It's made in China, of course!
  What exactly is the drink made of?

- *Make* is used in calculations.
  That makes a total of $46 altogether.

- *Make* is used to talk about arrangements and meetings.
  Can you make it on Thursday?
  Hi, Alain. I'm glad you made it.

Do

- *Do* is used as a main verb to talk about activities.
  It's good to be near the government offices because we do a lot of work with them.
  A company called AR Surveys is doing research into tiredness at work.

- *Do* is often used with –*ing* nouns.
  The tour leader asked me to do the cooking.

What's your job?

• You can ask and answer questions about jobs like this.

What's your job? = What do you do?
– I'm a futurologist.

I'm a/an | *accountant*
designer
engineer
factory worker
manager
office worker
researcher
salesman/saleswoman/salesperson
secretary

Who do you work for?
– I work for Global Credit Bank.
Where do you work?

– I work | *in a factory/office/shop/showroom/TV studio.*
at the head office.

Which department do you work in?

– I work in the | *sales* | *department.*
accounts
human resources
production
planning
marketing

Or:
I work in sales.
I work in accounts.

• You can talk about companies and what they do like this.
What does your company/organization do?
– We make computers. = We manufacture computers.
– We produce video games in 10 languages.
– We offer financial services.
– We make and sell television programmes.
– It/the company distributes soft drinks.

Core business vocabulary

• Here is a list of important business words. Do you know them all? Can you use them?

accounts	advertising	asset	brand (n)	budget (n)
cash (n)	charge (v)	client	compete	competition
contract	currency	customer	debt	discount
distribute	distribution	distributor	economic	economy
export (n + v)	finance (n + v)	financial	goods	group
import (n + v)	industry	insurance	interest	invest
investment	invoice (n + v)	loan (n)	loss	manage
management	manager	market (n)	office	order
packaging	plant	product	profit	profitable
program	range	recruit (n + v)	refund (n + v)	retail (n + v)
retailing	retailer	sales	ship (n + v)	shipping
software	stock (n + v)	supplier	supply (n + v)	warehouse (n)

Word combinations: *product*

- Word combinations are very important in Business English. These adjectives come in front of *product* in *Best Practice Pre-intermediate*.

a/an	new	product
	food	
	beauty	
	pharmaceutical	
	efficient	
	successful	
	reliable	

- Here are some verbs used in front of *product*.

design	
develop	
manufacture	a product
market	
launch	
sell	
buy	

What's the secret for making and marketing a successful product?
– We're a big European distributor of pharmaceutical products.

Word combinations: adjectives and nouns

- Here are some adjectives and nouns that may go together.

economic growth   electronic goods   industrial group

Word combinations: noun and noun

- Now look at some nouns that may go together.

distribution channel   insurance policy
export market   time management
import agent

Word combinations: nouns and verbs

- Look at these examples of verbs that can typically come in front of some of the nouns from the core business vocabulary above.

pay cash	give a discount
find a distributor	find a distributor
obtain finance	increase sales
develop software	

- Now look at nouns that typically follow some of the verbs from the core business vocabulary.

import goods	invest money
invoice a customer	manage a team
recruit a new manager	stock goods

Business vocabulary in context

- Look at how these two speakers use typical combinations.

At Medexquip, we make medical equipment. We are based in the Netherlands – our **manufacturing plant** and **head office** are here. Our **main customers** are hospitals, mostly in Europe and North America, but we have also **entered the market** in Asia, and we are **increasing our market share** there. We have some very **important customers** there now. We've **recruited a new sales manager** and **she goes on business trips** to Asia four times a year. It usually takes three or four visits before a **customer signs a contract**. But after that, they usually stay with us for a very long time!

I've bought from Medexquip for 10 years now. They're a very **reliable supplier**. They have **high prices** compared to their competitors, but the equipment is **very high quality**. I've visited the **research centre** near Amsterdam where they **design** and **develop products** – very interesting! When Medexquip's sales manager comes to visit, they always have something new to show us. Their **range** is very **wide**. There's always something new in their **product catalogue** that I want to buy. Sometimes we have **difficult negotiations**, but we usually sign a new contract in the end!

Marketing manager

Hospital director

Telephone/e-mail language

Asking for someone
Is that Asafla Travel?
Can I speak to Maya Nolan, please?
Can I speak to someone in R and D?
Can I speak to someone who deals with distribution?

Saying who you are
Hello Amanda. This is Zak.
Daljit, hello. (It's) Susan here.
I'm calling from AR Surveys.

Asking for the caller's name
Who's calling, please?
How do you spell your name, please?
Can you say that again, please?

Asking the caller to wait
Hold on, please.
Hold the line, please.
Please hold.
A: *Would you like to hold?*
B: *OK. I'll hold. / No, thanks. I'll call back later.*

Offering help
Sorry to keep you waiting.
Can I help?
How can I help?
What can I do for you?

Asking if it's a good time to call
A: *Sorry to call you so late. Am I disturbing you? Is this a good time to call?*
B: *Well, actually, this isn't a very good time. I'm preparing a presentation. Could I call you tomorrow?*

If the person is not available
Sorry – the line's busy.
I'm sorry, buts he isn't here today.
Daljit Khan is in a meeting/out of the office/on holiday.
Can I take a message? / Would you like to leave a message?

Leaving a message
Can you give her a message?
I'm phoning about ...
Can she call me tomorrow, please?
Can you ask her to call me back?
Can she send me an e-mail?
I have a problem for our meeting on Wednesday afternoon. Can she call me back so we can fix another time?

Confirming details
A: *My name's Jones.*
B: *How do you spell that?*
A: *Jones. J-O-N-E-S.*
B: *Can you confirm the first line of your address?*
A: *32 London Road.*
B: *32 London Road?*
A: *That's right. / That's it.*

Telephone alphabet
- If you want to spell a word, you can say, for example, 'C for Charlie' or 'C as in Charlie'. This list shows words often used for this, but you can use your own names or words.

Apple	**H**otel	**O**scar	**V**ictor
Bravo	**I**ndia	**P**apa	**W**hisky
Charlie	**J**uliet	**Q**uebec	**X**-ray
Delta	**K**ilo	**R**omeo	**Y**ankee
Echo	**L**ima	**S**ierra	**Z**ulu
Foxtrot	**M**ike	**T**ango	
Golf	**N**ovember	**U**niform	

Phone numbers

00　1　212　734　892
oh-oh one two-one-two seven-three-four eight-nine-two

3020
three-oh-two-oh

zero-zero one two-one-two seven-three-four eight-nine-two
three-zero-two-zero

744　　　　2899
seven-double-four　two-eight-double-nine

seven-four-four　　two-eight-nine-nine

E-mail addresses
Write: alain.bonneval@softgames.fr
Say:　A-L-A-I-N dot B-O-double N-E-V-A-L – at softgames – softgames all one word – dot F-R

Countries, adjectives, capitals

European Union

Country	Adjective	Capital
Austria	Austrian	Vienna
Belgium	Belgian	Brussels
Cyprus	Cypriot	Nicosia
Czech Republic	Czech	Prague
Denmark	Danish	Copenhagen
Estonia	Estonian	Tallinn
Finland	Finnish	Helsinki
France	French	Paris
Germany	German	Berlin
Greece	Greek	Athens
Hungary	Hungarian	Budapest
Ireland	Irish	Dublin
Italy	Italian	Rome
Latvia	Latvian	Riga
Lithuania	Lithuanian	Vilnius
Luxembourg	—	Luxembourg
Malta	Maltese	Valetta
Netherlands	Dutch	The Hague
Portugal	Portuguese	Lisbon
Slovakia	Slovakian	Bratislava
Slovenia	Slovenian	Ljubljana
Spain	Spanish	Madrid
Sweden	Swedish	Stockholm
Poland	Polish	Warsaw
United Kingdom*	—	London

*Countries of the UK

England	English	London
Wales	Welsh	Cardiff
Scotland	Scottish	Edinburgh
Northern Ireland	Northern Irish	Belfast

England + Wales + Scotland = Great Britain.
The adjective = British.

Some other European countries

Switzerland	Swiss	Berne
Norway	Norwegian	Oslo
Russia**	Russian	Moscow

**Of course, a lot of Russia is in Asia!

Some Asian countries

Country	Adjective	Capital
China	Chinese	Beijing
India	Indian	New Delhi
Japan	Japanese	Tokyo
Malaysia	Malaysian	Kuala Lumpur
Pakistan	Pakistani	Islamabad
Taiwan	Taiwanese	Taipei
Indonesia	Indonesian	Jakarta
Philippines	Philippine	Manila
Singapore	Singaporean	Singapore
South Korea	South Korean	Seoul

Australasia

Australia	Australian	Canberra
New Zealand	—	Auckland

Some North African countries

Morocco	Moroccan	Rabat
Tunisia	Tunisian	Tunis
Egypt	Egyptian	Cairo

Some other African countries

Kenya	Kenyan	Nairobi
Nigeria	Nigerian	Abuja
South Africa	South African	Pretoria

North America

Canada	Canadian	Quebec
United States	American	Washington, DC

Some countries in Latin America

Argentina	Argentinean	Buenos Aires
Brazil	Brazilian	Brasilia
Chile	Chilean	Santiago
Mexico	Mexican	Mexico City

Grammar overview

Verbs

Present simple

be

Affirmative	Negative	Questions
I'm (am).	I'm not (am not).	Am I?
You're (are).	You aren't (are not).	Are you?
He	He	he?
She 's (is).	She isn't (is not).	Is she?
It	It	it?
We're (are).	We aren't (are not).	Are we?
They're (are).	They aren't (are not).	Are they?

Regular verbs

Affirmative	Negative	Questions
I work.	I don't (do not) work.	Do I work?
You work.	You don't (do not) work.	Do you work?
He	He	he
She works.	She doesn't (does not) work.	Does she work?
It	It	it
We work.	We don't (do not) work.	Do we work?
They work.	They don't (do not) work.	Do they work?

Form

- For *be* and regular verbs, see above.
- With *go* and *do*, and with verbs ending in *-ch*, *-ss*, *-sh* and *-x*, add *-es* to the base form of the verb.
  Chanel no. 5 never goes out of fashion.
  1995: Stelios launches easyJet.

***Wh-* questions**

- With *I, you, we, they*, you make *Wh-* questions with *do*.
  Why do you think your investment will be more profitable than the others?
- With *he/she/it*, you make *Wh-* questions with *does*.
  What does Clara Rios do?

Use

You use the present simple:

- to talk about general facts.
  Jennifer Powell works in Singapore for the Global Credit Bank.
- to talk about customs, habits and routines.
  The exhibition closes at 11.
- to talk about personal characteristics.
  She likes comfortable armchairs.
- to describe processes.
  We interview nine or ten people. Then we interview two or three of them again and offer the job to the best person.

Present continuous

Affirmative	Negative	Questions
I'm (am) working.	I'm not (am not) working.	Am I working?
You're (are) working.	You aren't (are not) working.	Are you working?
He	He	he
She 's (is) working.	She isn't (is not) working.	Is she working?
It	It	it
We're (are) working.	We aren't (are not) working.	Are we working?
They're (are) working.	They aren't (are not) working.	Are they working?

Form

- You make the present continuous with *be* + the *-ing* form of the verb.

To make the *-ing* form of the verb:

- most regular verbs: add *-ing* to the base form of the verb
  do – doing
  think – thinking

- verbs ending in *-e*: drop the *-e* and add *-ing*
  drive – driving
  hope – hoping
  taste – tasting

- verbs ending in a vowel and a consonant: double the consonant and add *-ing*
  hit – hitting
  win – winning

- verbs ending in a vowel or *-y* or *-w*: add *-ing*
  ski – skiing
  play – playing

Question words

You make questions with question words like this.

How are you paying?   What is he doing?   Where is she going?

Use

You use the present continuous:

- to talk about what is happening now.
  Taro is singing in a karaoke bar.
- to talk about present trends.
  People are living longer, healthier lives.
- to talk about temporary situations.
  It's difficult to park because they're working on the road.
  (You can say this in the evening too, when the work has stopped for the day.)
- to talk about future plans that are quite certain, for example travel plans.
  I'm flying back home tomorrow evening.

Past simple

be

Affirmative	Negative	Questions
I was.	I wasn't (was not).	Was I?
You were.	You weren't (were not).	Were you?
He	He	he?
She was.	She wasn't (was not).	Was she?
It	It	it?
We were.	We weren't (were not).	Were we?
They were.	They weren't (were not).	Were they?

Regular verbs

Affirmative		Negative		Questions		
I You He She It We They	worked.	I You He She It We They	didn't (did not) work.	Did	I you he she it we they	work?

Form

- Most regular verbs: add *-ed* to the base form of the verb.
    talk – talked
    work – worked
- Verbs ending in *-e*: add *-d*.
    hope – hoped
    decide – decided
- Verbs of one syllable ending in a vowel and a consonant: double the consonant and add *-ed*.
    plan – planned
    stop – stopped
- Verbs ending in *-y*: drop the *-y* and add *-ied*.
    carry – carried   study – studied
- Verbs ending in a vowel + *-y*: add *-ed*.
    delay – delayed
    play – played
- For irregular past simple forms, see page 000.

Question words

You make questions with question words like this.
    Where did you go?   What did you see?   How much did you pay to get in?

Pronunciation

/t/   *talked, stopped, worked*
/d/   *agreed, listened, moved*
/ɪd/ (past simple endings *-ded* and *-ted*)
    decided   needed   invested   wanted

Use

You use the past simple:
- to talk about events in the past.
    Did they find enough developers? – No, they didn't. They needed 50 and they only found 20.
- to give a specific time for an event in the past. For example, you always use it with:
    at (3 o'clock)   yesterday   last week   last month
    The software writing stage started two months late and only finished last month.
- with *ago*:
    How long ago did Stelios leave easyJet?
    He left the company three years ago.

Present perfect

Affirmative			Negative			Questions		
I You	have		I You	haven't (have not)		Have	I you	
He She It	has	worked.	He She It	hasn't (has not)	worked.	Has	he she it	worked?
We They	have		We They	haven't		Have	we they	

Form

- You make the present perfect with *have* or *has* + the past participle of the verb.

To make regular past participles:

- most regular verbs ending in *-e*: add *-d*
  decide – decided
  state – stated
- most regular verbs ending in a consonant followed by *-y*: drop the *y* and add *-ied*
  deny – denied
  empty – emptied
- most other regular verbs: add *-ed*
  talk – talked
  play – played
- For irregular past participles, see page 000.

Use

You use the present perfect:

- to talk about recent events.
  Bertrand Delanoë has done a lot to help.
  The photocopier has broken down. Can you call the technician?
- to talk about past events, without mentioning a specific time, for example with *ever* and *never*.
  Paris has some of the best public transport of any city I have ever lived in or visited.
  Visitor numbers to American museums have never been higher.
- to say that something has happened, for example with *already*.
  We've already finished the designs ...
- to say that something has not happened, for example in the negative with *yet*.
  ... but we haven't started production yet.
- to talk about an activity that started in the past and is still continuing, for example with *since* + points in time and *for* + periods of time.
  Lauren has been a freelancer since 1998.
  She has studied Spanish for 6 months.

Past continuous

Affirmative			Negative			Questions		
I was You were			I wasn't You weren't			Was I Were you		
He She It	was	working.	He She It	wasn't	working.	Was	he she it	working?
We They	were		We They	weren't		Were	we they	

Form

- You form the past continuous with *was/were* and the *–ing* form of the verb.

Use

- You use the past continuous to talk about something that was in progress when something else happened.

    We were preparing to launch the product when there was a fire in the factory.

Future with *going to*

- You use *going to* and the base form of the verb to talk about future plans and intentions.

    Russia is going to be an important market for us.
    We're going to recruit fifty software developers.

Future with *will*

Affirmative			Negative			Questions		
I You He She It We They	'll (will)	work.	I You He She It We They	won't (will not)	work.	Will	I you he she it you they	work?

Form

- You make the future simple with *will* and the base form of the verb.

Question words

You make questions with question words like this.

    How much will it cost?

Use

You use *will*:

- to talk about future events.

    People will spend less time at work.

- to talk about a decision you make at the time of speaking.

    She's out of the office, so I'll call her on her mobile.

Modal verbs

- Here are some modal verbs.

    can   could   may   must   will   would   should

Form

Modal verbs:

- don't change their form for different persons.
    Can she speak Italian?
    Could you help me with these figures?

- are not used with *do* in questions and negatives.
    Could we have another bottle of wine?
    Customers won't like this product.

- are followed by the base form of the verb without *to*.
    You must finish that by this evening.
    Would you take my bags upstairs?

can – use

You use *can:*

- to talk about possibilities.
  Our salesman can come on Wednesday morning.
- to make offers.
  Can I help you?
- to ask for things.
  Can you give me your name, please?

You use *can't* to talk about things you are:

- not able to do.
  We can't deliver before next year.
- not allowed to do.
  You can't smoke in here.

could – use

You use *could:*

- to ask for something politely.
  Could I have the bill please?
- to ask people to do things.
  Could you get me a coffee, please?
- to make predictions: see below.

must and should – use

- You use *must* and *should* to tell someone what to do. *Must* is stronger than *should.*
  You must arrive between 7 and 7.30.
  You should take a week off work.
- You use *mustn't (must not)* and *shouldn't (should not)* to tell someone what not to do. *Mustn't* is stronger than *shouldn't.*
  You must not smoke in here.
  You shouldn't try to deal with stress by drinking alcohol.
- You can use *should* in questions to ask for advice.
  What should I do? Should I call an ambulance?

don't have to and needn't – use

- You use *don't have to* and *needn't* to say that something is not necessary.
  You don't have to give your name, but you can if you want to.
  You needn't arrive early. We don't start till 10.

will, might, may and could for predictions

- You use *will* to say that you think that something in the future is quite certain.
  In 2050, English will still be the most important language for international communication.
- You use *might, may* or *could* to say that it is possible, but not certain, that something will happen in the future.
  In 2050, there might be a cure for cancer.
  Climate change may mean that it is too hot for holidays in the Mediterranean.
  All work could be done at home – there could be no need for office buildings.

Passive

Form

- You form the passive with *is/are* or *was/were* + the past participle of the verb.
  Research is done at the research centre in New York State.
  Production was lost because of workers off sick.

To make regular past participles:

- most regular verbs ending in *-e*: add *-d*
  decide – decided
  state – stated

- most regular verbs ending in a consonant followed by -y: drop the y and add -ied
  deny – denied
  empty – emptied
- most other regular verbs: add -ed
  talk – talked
  play – played
- For irregular past participles, see page 104.

Use

- You use the passive to talk about something affected by an action.
  Where were these trees planted?
  The exhibition was sponsored by a fashion magazine.

First conditional

Form

- You form the first conditional with the present simple tense in the *If*-clause and *will* in the main clause.
  If you need to work at home, we'll provide the technology.

Use

- You use the first conditional to talk about possibilities.
  If you buy 200,000 units, the unit price will be $19.
  If we make this investment, will we get 3 million visitors a year.

Second conditional

Form

- You form the second conditional with the past simple tense in the *If*-clause and *would* in the main clause.
  If public transport improved, would you use it more?

Use

- You can use the second conditional to talk about situations that are not likely to happen soon.
  If there was a day without cars in your area, would you stay at home?
  – Yes, I would. / No, I wouldn't. I'd cycle to work.

Verb patterns

Some verbs follow particular patterns. For example:

- to ask someone (not) to do something.
  She asked them not to miss the meeting.
- to tell someone (not) to do something.
  I told Mr Lee to come back with a better offer.
- to advise someone (not) to do something.
  His lawyer advised him to read the contract carefully.
- to want someone to do something.
  I wanted him to go away and think about it.
- to agree with someone (about something).
  Management agreed with employees about the need for better training.
- to disagree with someone (about something).
  He disagreed with the supplier about the delivery dates.

Verbs with prepositions and particles

- Some verbs are used with prepositions.
  Listen to the conversation.

- Sometimes the meaning of a verb changes when it is used with a preposition or a particle. Compare these two sentences.
  I dropped the cup on the floor and it broke.
  You're breaking up – I can't hear you.

- Here are some verb + particle combinations with an object. Notice how you can change the word order.
  I picked my baggage up. I picked up my baggage.
  I turned on the heating and then turned it off.

- But you must put object pronouns (for example *it*) between the verb and the particle.
  I picked it up.

- In the case of verb + preposition combinations with an object you cannot change the word order.
  The meeting quickly went through the minutes.

Irregular verbs

Base form	Past tense	Past participle	Base form	Past tense	Past participle
be	was/were	been	lie	lay	lain
become	became	become	lost	lost	lost
begin	began	begun	make	made	made
break	broke	broken	mean	meant	meant
bring	brought	brought	meet	met	met
build	built	built	pay	paid	paid
buy	bought	bought	quit	quit	quit
catch	caught	caught	read	read	read
choose	chose	chosen	ride	rode	ridden
come	came	come	ring	rang	rung
cost	cost	cost	rise	rose	risen
cut	cut	cut	run	ran	run
deal	dealt	dealt	say	said	said
do	did	done	see	saw	seen
draw	drew	drawn	sell	sold	sold
drink	drank	drunk	send	sent	sent
drive	drove	driven	set	set	set
eat	ate	eaten	shake	shook	shaken
fall	fell	fallen	shoot	shot	shot
feel	felt	felt	show	showed	shown
find	found	found	shut	shut	shut
fly	flew	flown	sing	sang	sung
forbid	forbade	forbidden	sit	sat	sat
forget	forgot	forgotten	sleep	slept	slept
get	got	got	speak	spoke	spoken
give	gave	given	spend	spent	spent
go	went	gone	spread	spread	spread
grow	grew	grown	stand	stood	stood
have	had	had	steal	stole	stolen
hear	heard	heard	stick	stuck	stuck
hide	hid	hidden	swim	swam	swum
hit	hit	hit	take	took	taken
hold	held	held	teach	taught	taught
hurt	hurt	hurt	tell	told	told
keep	kept	kept	think	thought	thought
know	knew	known	throw	threw	thrown
lay	laid	laid	understand	understood	understood
lead	led	led	wear	wore	worn
learn	learnt/learned	learnt/learned	win	won	won
leave	left	left	write	wrote	written
lend	lent	lent			
let	let	let			

Nouns

Plurals

Regular

- Most nouns: add -s.
    - *car – cars*
    - *product – products*
- Nouns ending in -y: drop the -y and add -ies.
    - *country – countries*
    - *city – cities*
- Nouns ending in -o, -ch, -ss, -sh, -x: add -es.
    - *branch – branches*
    - *crash – crashes*

Irregular

- *man – men*
- *child – children*
- *person – people*
- *woman – women*

Count and uncount nouns

- Some nouns are count nouns. They have plural forms, as shown above.
    - *1 brand – 2 brands, 1 company – 2 companies*
    - *1 woman – 2 women, 1 child – 2 children*
- Other nouns are uncount. They do not have a plural.
    - *work   money   free time*
- Some nouns can be both count and uncount.
    - *I believe in the importance of good design.*
    - *The clients did not like the architect's designs.*
- Some nouns can only be uncount. Here are some of them:
    - *advice   employment   equipment   furniture   homework*
    - *information knowledge   money   progress   traffic*

Other structures with nouns

a/an

- You use *a*:
    - — in front of nouns that begin with a consonant.
        - *a warehouse*
    - — in front of adjectives before nouns where the adjective begins with a consonant.
        - *a hi-tech office*
- You use *an*:
    - — in front of nouns that begin with a vowel.
        - *an activity*
    - — in front of adjectives before nouns where the adjective begins with a vowel.
        - *an inefficient organisation*
- You use *a/an* when you talk about something for the first time.
    - *You have a budget of $4 million.*
    - *I'm busy – I'm in an interview.*
- You use *a/an* with jobs.
    - *He's a coffee grower.*
    - *She's a professor of chemistry.*

the

- You use *the*:
    - — to talk about something again.
        - *The project is behind schedule.*
    - — when there is only one.
        - *The game design stage went OK.*

there is / there are

- With singular and uncount nouns, you use *there is* or *there's* in spoken English.
  Is there a business that doesn't have effects on the environment?
  There's too much furniture.
  There is one wrong word.
  There's a train strike.
  There's another delay.

- With plural nouns you use *there are*.
  There are more than 500 theme parks in the US.
  Analyse why there are losses.
  Are there other facilities?
  There are four types of remote working.
  There are technical reasons and there are also the human factors.
  There are 50 bike rack spaces in all.

- For *there is / there are + some* or *any*, see below.

much/many/a lot

- With count nouns, you ask questions with *How many*.
  How many visitors will there be?
  How many tickets would you like?
  How many hours a week do you work?
  How many jobs have you had?

- You can answer with:
  — a number: *3 million.   Four.   39.   Five.*
  — or with: *Not many.   Not a lot.   A lot.*

- With uncount nouns, you ask questions with *How much*.
  How much tea and coffee do you drink?
  How much profit you expect to make?
  How much progress has been made?

- You can answer with:
  — a quantity: *Four cups.   10 million.*
  — or with: *Not much.   Not a lot.   A lot.*

- You can also use *a lot* as an adverb.
  I like it a lot.

some and **any**

- You usually use *some* with uncount nouns and with plural count nouns to talk about a quantity of something without being exact.

- You use *some* in affirmative sentences, but not in negative sentences.
  I'd like to order some Avgard furniture.
  Some trends for the next 50 years are already becoming clear.

- You can use *some* in questions – for example, when you ask for something or offer something.
  Could you give me some advice?
  Would you like some juice?

- You use *any* in questions and negative sentences.
  Were there any downsides to your visit?
  Have you made any calculations?
  We haven't made any final decisions.
  No one took any notice of the bus lanes.

Adjectives

Possessive adjectives

I → *my*   you → *your*   he → *his*   she → *her*   it → *its*   we → *our*   they → *their*
  They're talking about their boss.

Comparatives and superlatives

- Adjectives with one syllable: add *-er* for the comparative and *-est* for the superlative.
  cheap – cheaper – cheapest
  thick – thicker – thickest
- Adjectives ending in *-e*: add *-r* for the comparative and *-st* for the superlative.
  fine – finer – finest
  wide – wider – widest
- Adjectives ending in *-y*: add *-ier* for the comparative and *-iest* for the superlative.
  healthy – healthier - healthiest
  ugly – uglier - ugliest
- One-syllable adjectives: double the consonant and add *-er* or *-est*.
  hot – hotter – hottest
  sad – sadder – saddest
- Two syllables or more, not ending in *-y*: use *more* for the comparative form and *most* for the superlative form of adjectives.
  efficient – more efficient – most efficient
  reliable – more reliable – most reliable
- Some comparative and superlative forms are irregular.
  good – better – best
  bad – worse – worst
- You use *than* (not *that*) to make comparisons.
  Anita's office is better than mine.
- Some adjectives do not have comparative and superlative forms.
  excellent   wonderful

Adverbs

- You usually make an adverb by adding *-ly* to the adjective.
  bad – badly
  usual – usually
- With adjectives ending in *-y*: drop the *-y* and add *-ily*.
  easy – easily
  funny – funnily
- Some adverbs are the same as the adjective.
  early   late   fast   hard
- Some adverbs are irregular.
  good – well
  Some museums are doing very well.

Comparatives and superlatives

- The comparatives and superlatives of adverbs are usually formed with *more* and *most*.
  easily – more easily – most easily
  efficiently – more efficiently – most efficiently
- Adverbs that have the same form as adjectives have the same comparatives and superlatives as the adjectives. See above.
- Some adverbs have comparatives and superlatives with *more* and *most* and also with *-er* and *-est*.
  quickly – more quickly – most quickly
  quick – quicker – quickest
- Some comparative and superlative forms are irregular.
  well – better – best
  badly – worse – worst

Word order

- Adverbs of frequency *always, often, sometimes, usually, never* go before the verb.
  People usually think that stress is a bad thing.
- But you put them after *be*.
  Her desk is always in a complete mess.

Audio script

Module 1 World of Work

Unit 1 A working day

1.1 **Conversation 1**

A: Cafés Pessoa.

B: Can I speak to Mr Pessoa, please?

A: He's at the warehouse this morning. You can call him there if you like.

B: OK. I have the number. Bye.

A: Bye.

Conversation 2

A: Galeries Beaumarchais, bonjour.

B: Monique Miller, please?

A: She's out to lunch. Can I take a message?

B: That's OK. I'll call her on her mobile.

A: OK. Good bye.

B: Bye.

Conversation 3

Vish: Hello, Vish speaking.

A: May I speak to Daljit Khan, please?

Vish: I'm afraid she's in a meeting. Can you call back later?

A: OK. I'll send her an e-mail. Thanks anyway.

Vish: No problem. Bye.

A: Bye.

Conversation 4

Taro: Hello.

Alan: Taro, hi, it's Alan.

Taro Alan, hi.

Alan: Sorry to call you so late.

Taro: That's all right.

Alan: Where are you?

Taro: I'm in a karaoke bar.

Unit 2 I spend all my time in meetings

2.1 1

Woman: I like to think I'm a fairly organised sort of person. I find I can think more clearly if I keep my desk tidy. I try to be nice to people – colleagues and customers. I think I get on well with people.

2

Man: People say that I'm good with detail – it saves a lot of time later if you can get everything right from the start. I'm quite good with computers – I don't see how you can be efficient without one. I try to be punctual for meetings – I think it's polite not to keep people waiting.

2.2 1

Woman: She's always in a bad mood. She doesn't get on very well with people – sometimes she's even quite rude to customers. She's very untidy – her desk is always in a complete mess – I don't know how she finds anything. She's so disorganised!

2

Man: I don't know how he got his job - he's hopeless with computers. He's not very good with detail – he's quite careless and makes a lot of mistakes. And he's always late for meetings. He's so inefficient!

2.3 **On the Line**

Conversation 1

Daljit: Hello.

Peter: Hello. Can I speak to Daljit, please?

Daljit: Speaking.

Peter: Hi, Daljit. It's Peter. Is this a good time to call?

Daljit: Not really. I'm in a meeting. Can I call you back later?

Peter: OK. Talk to you later.

Daljit: Bye.

Peter: Bye.

Conversation 2

Daljit: Hello, Daljit speaking.

Susan: Daljit, hello. Susan here. Am I disturbing you?

Daljit: Well... this isn't a very good time. I'm preparing a presentation.

Susan: Could I call you later?

Daljit: OK. I'll be at home all evening. Bye for now.

Susan: Bye.

Conversation 3

Daljit: Hello!

Ravi: Daljit, it's Ravi. It doesn't sound like a good time to call.

Daljit: Well, no, it isn't actually. I'm rather busy – I'm in an interview.

Ravi: OK. Maybe it's easier if I send you an e-mail.

Daljit: OK – I'll look out for it. Sorry I can't talk now. Bye.

Ravi: Bye.

Unit 3 We're behind schedule

3.1 *Daljit:*

OK. I'm going to talk about the project development schedule for our new video game Crazy Raiders. We're working with a UK company on the project. Over the next three months, our partners in the UK will finalise the design of the game itself. Meanwhile, in Bangalore, over July and August, we're going to recruit fifty software developers to write the software for the project – they're going to work for eight months from September. Back in the UK, they're going to do the design of the packaging from January to May next year. We're going to manufacture the product in China next year, from May onwards. The big day is in autumn next year – we're going to launch the product on the first of September, on time and on budget!

3.2 On the line

Daljit: Hello.

Keith: Hi, Daljit. It's Keith. Thanks for your memo.

Daljit: Hello, Keith. You got it OK, then?

Keith: Yes, and I'm rather worried about the delays. Why didn't you tell me about them before?

Daljit: I didn't want to bother you – we're going to launch on time, that's the main thing.

Keith: Maybe, but the schedule's very tight. And we don't have the level of stocks that we wanted. If customers come into the shops and can't buy the product it's a disaster!

Daljit: Keith, don't worry. We'll have enough stocks – the manufacturers are working overtime.

Keith: Yes, but they're charging us more because of the rush. I guess that's one of the things that means we're over budget.

Daljit: Yes, but don't panic! The project is going to be a big success. Crazy Raiders is going to be a very profitable product!

Keith: Maybe. The main reason I'm phoning is because I want to talk about the budget …

Daljit: OK.

Unit 4 Are you a team player?

4.1 On the line

Conversation 1

Brenda: Hello.

Alex: Brenda, it's Alex. Where's the delivery we're waiting for from Rapid Office Supplies? Their delivery people said this morning, before midday.

Brenda: Didn't you get the message? They phoned yesterday. The goods aren't ready. They're delivering them next week instead.

Alex: No one told me. I need those supplies urgently for a project that I'm working on.

Conversation 2

Denise: Hello, Denise here.

Caroline: Denise, hi, it's Caroline. I'm in the meeting room for our weekly meeting. But there's no one here.

Denise: Didn't they tell you? This week's meeting is cancelled. But we're meeting next week as usual.

Caroline: Oh no! No one tells me anything! I left home early just to be here.

Conversation 3

Ed: Hello.

Fabrizio: Hello, Ed. It's Fabrizio here. I'm phoning about the report. The deadline was yesterday, you know.

Ed: Yesterday? You told me it was next week.

Fabrizio: Yes, but the boss says it's a rush job. She wants it now.

Ed: Why didn't you tell me before?

Conversation 4

Gary: Gary Chambers.

Helena: Gary, it's Helena. Our visitor's waiting in reception – you know, Mr Conway.

Gary: But his appointment is tomorrow, not today.

Helena: We changed the appointment to today. I sent you an e-mail this morning. Didn't you get it?

Gary: I don't know. I didn't check my e-mails. I'm sorry, Helena.

I can't see him today. Can you see him and tell me what you decide?

Helena: OK. But I wanted you to be there – it's important.

4.2 Conversation 1

Brenda: Hello.

Alex: Brenda, it's Alex. Where's the delivery we're waiting for from Rapid Office Supplies? Their delivery people said this morning, before midday.

Brenda: Didn't you get the message? They phoned yesterday. The goods aren't ready. They're delivering them next week instead.

Alex: No one told me. I need those supplies urgently for a project that I'm working on.

Brenda: I phoned you late yesterday afternoon but there was no reply. I left a message - I guess you'd already gone home.

Alex: Yes, I left a bit early yesterday …

Conversation 2

Denise: Hello, Denise here.

Caroline: Denise, hi, it's Caroline. I'm in the meeting room for our weekly meeting. But there's no one here.

109

Denise: Didn't they tell you? This week's meeting is cancelled. But we're meeting next week as usual.

Caroline: Oh no! No one tells me anything! I left home early just to be here.

Denise: I tried to phone you at home this morning, but you'd already left.

Caroline: Yes, the phone rang just as I was going out of the door, but I was in a hurry to get to the meeting ...

Denise: Oh no ...

Conversation 3

Ed: Hello.

Fabrizio: Hello, Ed. It's Fabrizio here. I'm phoning about the report. The deadline was yesterday, you know.

Ed: Yesterday? You told me it was next week.

Fabrizio: Yes, but the boss says it's a rush job. She wants it now.

Ed: Why didn't you tell me before?

Fabrizio: I've only just heard myself. You're the first person I've told.

Ed: This place is driving me crazy! Everything has to be done by yesterday ...

Conversation 4

Gary: Gary Chambers.

Helena: Gary, it's Helena. Our visitor's waiting in reception – you know, Mr Conway.

Gary: But his appointment is tomorrow, not today.

Helena: We changed the appointment to today. I sent you an e-mail this morning. Didn't you get it?

Gary: I don't know. I didn't check my e-mails. I'm sorry, Helena.

I can't see him today. Can you see him and tell me what you decide?

Helena: OK. But I wanted you to be there – it's important.

Gary: Just go ahead and see him – and let me know what happens.

Helena: OK, I'll let you know as soon as it's over.

Gary: Thanks, Helena ...

Module 2 The business of leisure

Unit 5 Staying in

5.1 *Speaker 1:*

I go for a traditional look. I like things to be cosy. I like elegant wallpaper and comfortable armchairs. I like thick carpets and heavy curtains to keep out the cold. We spend a lot on this house – we have new wallpaper and carpets every seven years or so. But every time, we stick to traditional designs with flowers. We have lots of

little tables around the room, so you have somewhere to put your cup of tea or glass of wine.

I don't like looking at electrical equipment all the time – it's so ugly. We put the television, the DVD player and the CD player in that wooden cabinet over there, and we open the doors when we want to watch TV. The television is 10 years old, and we've just bought a DVD player. We don't have a computer so we don't order on the internet – we drive to the department store in the city centre. The sales assistants there are so helpful!

Speaker 2:

You go into a typical house, and there's too much furniture. I want a house with clean lines, modern and hi-tech. There's no flowery wallpaper here. We don't have curtains, just these electrically operated blinds. We have a big plasma screen on the wall and these elegant loudspeakers – they sound as good as they look! People tell me that I don't have a lot of furniture, but that's the whole idea. I want things to look clean and minimalist.

I read a lot of technical magazines, so I know exactly what I want to buy. I usually buy on the internet – it's so easy to compare products and prices from different sellers. Sometimes I order by phone, but I never waste time driving into town. You've got to find somewhere to park, then you get into the shop and the product you want is out of stock. And the sales assistants just don't know what they're talking about.

5.2 **On the line**

Conversation 1

Emma: You're through to the order department. My name's Emma. How can I help?

Martin: Hello. I have your catalogue in front of me. I'd like to order some Avgard furniture. It's on page 55.

Emma: What would you like to order?

Martin: A sofa and two armchairs. They're available in white and grey, right?

Emma: Let me just check on the system.

Martin: OK.

Emma: We have everything in stock – both white and grey. We could deliver next Wednesday afternoon, if that's suitable.

Martin: Fine. I'll take them in white.

Emma: OK, two Avgard armchairs and one sofa, in white. They're guaranteed for 10 years, by the way.

Martin: Yes, I saw that in the catalogue.

Emma: Can you give me your name, please?

Martin: My name's Martin Barnes ...

5.3 **Conversation 2**

Emma: Order department. Emma speaking. What can I do for you?

Martin: Hello. I ordered some Avgard furniture from you last week. Was it you I spoke to?

Emma: Maybe. I take so many orders that I can't remember them all.

Martin: Anyway, the furniture arrived today and I'm not happy with it – I'd like to send it back and get a refund.

Emma: Why? Is there some kind of defect?

Martin: Well, no ... Actually, my wife doesn't like it ...

Emma: We can't give you a refund, but we can give you a credit note for when you buy something in the future ...

Martin: OK.

Emma: ... or you can exchange it for something else with the same value ...

Martin: I think I'll exchange it.

Emma: What's your name?

Martin: My name's Martin Barnes ...

Unit 6 Museums and exhibitions

6.1 On the line

Autoticket sales person: Autoticket. Can I help you?

Customer: Yes, I'd like some tickets for the *Speed* exhibition.

Autoticket sales person: Ah, *Speed*. It's a real blockbuster – it's booked solid. There's nothing available for three weeks.

Customer: Wow! OK ... Do you have anything available for Saturday March 30th?

Autoticket sales person: Yes, but in the evening only, from 6.30 on. Is that OK?

Customer: Fine. I'll take some tickets for 7.

Autoticket sales person: OK. You must arrive between 7 and 7.30, but you can stay as long as you like until the exhibition closes at 11. How many tickets would you like?

Customer: Two adults and two children.

Autoticket sales person: How old are the children?

Customer: One is 9 and the other 15.

Autoticket sales person: OK. Children over 14 pay full price, so that's three adults and one child. The regular price is 15 dollars for adults and 8 for children, but because you're going in the evening, it's 10 dollars for adults and 6 for children.

Customer: OK. That's good.

Autoticket sales person: So that makes a total of 46 dollars.

Customer: 46?! Just a moment. I think there's a mistake ...

Unit 7 Family entertainment

7.1 Conversation 1

Interviewer: Excuse me, ma'm, may I ask you a few questions? Where are you folks from?

Visitor 1: Of course. We're from Paris.

Interviewer: That's Paris, France, I guess, not Paris, Texas.

Visitor 1: That's right.

Interviewer: Did you folks have a good time here today at *Farwest*? What did you like the most?

Visitor 1: Yes, it was great. The kids loved those wild horses at the rodeo.

Interviewer: And was there anything you didn't like?

Visitor 1: Well, there was no wine at the Mexican restaurant at lunch time, only beer. I love Californian wine. I wanted some with my meal.

Interviewer: I'm sorry about that, ma'am. I'll let our management know.

Conversation 2

Interviewer: Excuse me, sir. May I ask you a few questions about your time here at *Farwest*? Did you have a good day?

Visitor 2: Sure.

Interviewer: Where are you from?

Visitor 2: Bangalore, in India. I'm here on vacation.

Interviewer: What did you like most here today?

Visitor 2: Well, I thought the lunch at the Delhi restaurant was excellent. Not exactly the Indian food we have in India, but very good. And I really liked the cowboy cooking demonstrations.

Interviewer: That's good to hear. Were there any downsides to your visit?

Visitor 2: Well, the lines at the roller coaster were very long. We had to wait half an hour to get on.

Interviewer: Yeah, that is a problem, especially in the middle of the day. But we're working on it. We're building another even bigger, better roller coaster.

Visitor 2: Right. I must try it when I come back next year.

Conversation 3

Interviewer: Excuse me, ma'm. Where are you from?

Visitor 3: From Liverpool, in England.

Interviewer: Did you have a good time here today?

Visitor 3: Yes, brilliant. We really liked the country music. It was so beautiful.

Interviewer: Was there anything that disappointed you?

Visitor 3: Well, as a matter of fact there was. There were no vegetarian options at the restaurant.

Interviewer: Which restaurant did you go to?

Visitor 3: The Big Steak restaurant.

Interviewer: But that's a meat restaurant!

7.2 On the line

Mary-Jane: Mary-Jane Lomax.

Taro: Hello Mary-Jane. This is Taro in Kyoto.

Mary-Jane:	Hi Taro. How are you today?
Taro:	Good. Mary-Jane, I want to talk about the latest visitor satisfaction scores. In front of me, I have...
Mary-Jane:	Before you go on, I know our overall score is very good...
Taro:	I wouldn't say that. I have the figures here in front of me, for all our theme parks.
Mary-Jane:	Right ... I know our score is 7.28 – that's not bad. And we got half a million visitors last year.
Taro:	Yes, but those are the lowest figures for all our theme parks!
Mary-Jane:	How can that be?
Taro:	Shark Paradise in Miami is our best-performing park. They got an overall score of 9.26. And they had two and a quarter million visitors last year.
Mary-Jane:	But that's impossible. There must be a mistake in the figures ...
Taro:	And some of the other parks did well too ... Let me give you all the figures.
Mary-Jane:	OK.
Taro:	Here in Japan, our Mountain Village park got 8.99, with one and half million visitors.
Mary-Jane:	Yes, but ...
Taro:	Let me just finish ... In France, Future City got 7.50 and had three quarters of a million visitors. In the UK, our Kings and Queens park had one and a quarter million visitors and obtained an overall score of 8.16. ...
Mary-Jane:	Just a moment, Taro. All those parks are newer than ours, with more modern equipment. Prices are lower. It's easier for them to get good staff. They're closer to other main tourist areas. Here in Utah, we're further away from the main tourist areas, for example on the west coast ...
Taro:	Maybe. But I want to discuss your figures with you. Can you come to Kyoto next week to talk about them, and above all, about improving them? How about Tuesday next week?
Mary-Jane:	OK. I'll ask my assistant to book a flight out on ...

Unit 8 Leisure in 2050

8.1 On the line

Taro:	Taro Suzuki.
Miranda Rees:	Hello Mr Suzuki. This is Miranda Rees at Crystal Ball Consultants in Geneva – we met at the New York Forum for the Future last year.
Taro:	Yes ...
Miranda Rees:	You remember we talked about long-term strategy. You said I could call you if I wanted to discuss long-term developments in the leisure industry.
Taro:	Ah, yes, I remember now. What would you like to know?
Miranda Rees:	For example, how do you see theme parks 50 years from now?
Taro:	I don't know about the next 50 years, but I can tell you about the next 10!
Miranda Rees:	OK.
Taro:	The industry will probably continue to grow 5 to 10 per cent a year. More and more people want to take their children somewhere special – the kids tell their parents to take them! Here at TS Leisure we have plans to open three more parks in the next ten years in Hong Kong, the US and Australia.
Miranda Rees:	Not Europe?
Taro:	Not enough children! In Europe, we're looking more and more at resorts for older people. We have no more plans for TS Leisure Club developments in the Mediterranean – we may close two or three of our existing 10 clubs. But we will open special clubs designed for older people – TS Leisure Senior Clubs.
Miranda Rees:	Right.
Taro:	Older people will want to spend long periods there, not only in summer but in winter too. We have only one club at the moment, but we have plans to build six more in the next ten years.
Miranda Rees:	And what about your film business?
Taro:	We'll probably continue to make films with actors for another 10 or 20 years – we make about three a year at the moment.
Miranda Rees:	Yes ...
Taro:	... but the future is digital. Of course, we make about five digital 'animated' films a year already, but computer power is growing so fast that soon we may not need actors at all.
Miranda Rees:	Aha ...
Taro:	We hope to produce 20 digital animated films a year, ten years from now, and only one or two with actors – they're so expensive and they can be so difficult to work with! We're investing heavily in animated films, using artists and programmers from all over the world at our centre in California.
Miranda Rees:	Really!
Taro:	Yes, we have great plans!

Module 3 Don't overdo it!

Unit 9 Getting fit

9.1 On the Line

Conversation 1

Dan: Dynamo Health Club.

Jennifer: Hi. My name's Jennifer Powell. I'm the human resources director for Global Credit Bank here in Singapore. We have 500 employees and they want to get fitter.

Dan: You've come to the right place! We offer corporate discounts on our normal fees.

Jennifer: How much are your normal fees?

Dan: The joining fee is 800 Singapore dollars and the annual fee after that is 3000 dollars.

Jennifer: What sort of discount can you give for our employees?

Dan: If you send a minimum of 50 people, we can give you 30 per cent on those rates.

Jennifer: OK, I'll think about that.

Dan: Would you like to come and see our facilities and discuss things further? We also have a café, a small supermarket ...

Jennifer: Let me think about the figures you gave me and I'll get back to you. Could I have your name, please?

Dan: Dan Foster.

Jennifer: OK, thanks Dan. Bye.

Dan: Bye.

Conversation 2

Erica: Elan Health Club, can I help you?

Jennifer: Hi. I'm phoning from Global Credit Bank. I'm the human resources director here – My name's Jennifer Powell. We have 500 employees and they want to get a lot fitter!

Erica: Right. Would you like to come over and see our facilities? Apart from the gym, we have a café, a supermarket, a doctor who's here every lunchtime ... Or I could come and see you in your office.

Jennifer: For the moment, could you just give me your fees? Do you offer corporate discounts?

Erica: Well, the normal joining fee is 500 Singapore dollars and the annual fee after that is 3500 dollars. But on those fees, we can offer a 25 per cent discount if you send at least 30 of your employees.

Jennifer: OK, I'll think about that.

Erica: Fine. Please get back to me if you require further information. I'm Erica Lee.

Jennifer: Thanks, Erica. I'll think about the figures you gave me and I'll get back to you.

Erica: OK, fine.

Jennifer: Bye.

Erica: Bye.

Conversation 3

Frank: Fun Health Club, good morning.

Jennifer: Hi. My name's Jennifer Powell. I'm the human resources director at Global Credit Bank. We have 500 employees and they want to get a lot fitter!

Frank: Right. We have a lot of corporate clients and we offer some very good deals. Our annual fee is 2000 dollars.

Jennifer: Your gym is cheaper than others that I've looked into.

Frank: Yes, we offer very competitive rates.

Jennifer: How much is the joining fee?

Frank: The basic fee is 450 dollars. And on those rates we offer 10 per cent discount if you enrol 40 or more employees.

Jennifer: I see. What are your facilities like?

Frank: We have a very well-equipped gym.

Jennifer: Do you have other facilities: a café, a supermarket ...?

Frank: No, we don't. They can go down the street for those. ...

Unit 10 Asleep on the job?

10.1 On the Line

Tommy: Hello.

Researcher: Hello. I'm calling from AR Surveys. We're doing research into tiredness at work. Do you have time to answer a few questions?

Tommy: How long will it take?

Researcher: Only a couple of minutes.

Tommy: OK. Fire away!

Researcher: How many hours a week do you work?

Tommy: Thirty-seven.

Researcher: Do you do shift work?

Tommy: No, I work normal office hours.

Researcher: When do feel at your best during the day?

Tommy: After lunch.

Researcher: And when do you feel at your worst?

Tommy: About an hour after I get to work: I feel exhausted.

Researcher: Can you tell me what you do for lunch? How long do you take for lunch?

Tommy: An hour. I think it's important to have a good break.

Researcher: What do you eat for lunch?

Tommy: Well, I usually go to my health club at lunchtime and I have a snack at the café there – soup and a salad, maybe, or a sandwich.

Researcher: Do you drink wine or beer with lunch?

Tommy: No, because if I do, I feel sleepy in the afternoon.

Researcher: How much tea and coffee do you drink during the day?

Tommy: I never drink tea. I don't like it. I have two cups of coffee for breakfast, two more when I get to work and a coffee after lunch. I don't drink coffee later in the day, because it keeps me awake at night, and I feel even more exhausted the next morning.

Researcher: OK. Thank you very much for your time.

Tommy: Not at all.

Unit 11 Dealing with stress

11.1

Interviewer: People usually think of stress as a bad thing. Is that always true?

Jennifer: Not always. We need stress in order to lead interesting lives, to motivate us to get up in the morning, go to work and so on. But too much stress is bad for us – it can lead to terrible feelings of anxiety, fear and anger.

Interviewer: Aha.

Jennifer: Stress can be caused by something negative like the death of a partner or losing your job. But it could even be something positive like a new partner or going on vacation.

Interviewer: Yes, I suppose you're right. I hadn't thought of that!

Jennifer: Anyway, it doesn't matter what the cause is, you shouldn't rely on caffeine or aspirin to keep you going, and you certainly shouldn't eat too much, or eat badly – you know, fast food, hamburgers, that sort of thing.

Interviewer: OK. What are the other things to avoid?

Jennifer: Well, you shouldn't try to deal with stress by drinking alcohol. That just makes it worse.

Interviewer: Right. Now – what do you do in your organisation to reduce stress among your employees?

Jennifer: Well, reducing stress among our staff is very important, so we give them space to relax while they're at work. There are special areas where they can relax, take a nap if they want to, play table football ...

Interviewer: Table football!

Jennifer: Yes, our employees love table football! But they have the chance to get real exercise too – we offer free membership at a health club near the bank. They can work out at the gym there.

Interviewer: Right ...

Jennifer: And in the evening our employees can go to art or music classes, learn a language,

whatever they like. The company pays for all this.

Interviewer: Wow!

Jennifer: Yes, as I said, we take the well-being of our staff very seriously ...

11.2 On the line

Sally: Human resources department. Sally Robinson speaking.

Tommy: Can I speak to the person who deals with absence?

Sally: I can deal with that. How can I help?

Tommy: My name's Tommy Chan.

Sally: Ah, here you are ... Chan, Tommy. You work in the back office here at headquarters, right?

Tommy: That's right. I'm phoning to say I can't come in today.

Sally: What's the problem?

Tommy: I went to the gym yesterday evening and I did something to my knee. I can hardly walk.

Sally: Oh, no. Have you been to see a doctor?

Tommy: Yes. She said I need to take at least a week off.

Sally: OK. Today's Thursday. Can we expect you back next Thursday?

Tommy: I don't know. I'm seeing the doctor again on Wednesday. I'll let you know after I see her.

Sally: OK. Give us another call then.

Tommy: OK. I'll talk to you next week. Bye for now.

Sally: Bye. Jennifer, that was another guy who's injured himself at the gym – the third one this month. He's taking at least a week off, maybe more.

Jennifer: Oh no, that gym idea may not be so good after all ...

Unit 12 Work-life balance

12.1 On the Line

Joanne: This is Joanne Samms.

Lauren: Oh, hello. I hope you don't mind if I call like this. My name's Lauren Charpentier. I sent you an application for a job as a web designer last week.

Joanne: Oh, hello!

Lauren: I'm calling to ask if you've had time to look at my application.

Joanne: Well, we have had a lot of applications. But yours is one of the most interesting. I was going to get in touch with you.

Lauren: Really! Thank you.

Joanne: Can you come in for an interview next week? How about Wednesday at 2?

Lauren: Can I get back to you? I have to find someone to look after my two-year-old daughter.

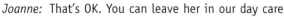

Joanne: That's OK. You can leave her in our day care centre during the interview.

Lauren: Oh good! Who should I ask for when I get there?

Joanne: Come to the reception desk and ask for me. I'll come down to meet you.

Lauren: Great. I look forward to meeting you!

Joanne: Me too. Bye for now.

Lauren: Thank you so much. Bye.

Module 4 New products, new markets

Unit 13 Low-cost airlines

13.1

1

A: I've just flown back from Nice in the south of France. I teach at Oxford and I was down there to see contacts at the university about a research project we're working on together. I paid £70 return. I think Quinnair is excellent. We left on time in both directions – that's the main thing. My satisfaction level? I give it 6 out of 7.

2

B: I've come from Spain, from Barcelona. My wife and I are retired – we have a house out there. My wife's there at the moment, but I had to come back to the UK to see my lawyers – can't tell you more than that! I paid £95 return – pretty good. Am I satisfied with Quinnair? Yes, it's not bad. OK, you have to pay for the sandwiches on board, but I wasn't hungry. I give it 5 out of 7.

3

C: I work in banking, for Global Credit Bank. I've been over to Geneva for a meeting at our branch there. The flight was slightly late going out yesterday, but right on time coming back, so I'm quite satisfied. But punctuality is what I'm most interested in. My score? 4 out of 7. Oh, and the fare: £84 return – very reasonable.

4

D: I've just come back from Prague. I went there on holiday with my girlfriend Zoë. We both work in a supermarket and we wanted to get away for a few days. Had a great time! There's so much to see and do, we didn't want to come back, but we have to get back to work tomorrow. Anyway, we paid £63 return and had a great time, so we're extremely satisfied: we give Quinnair 7 out of 7.

13.2 On the line

Dawn: Dawn speaking. How may I help?

Rebecca: I have a reservation to Barcelona on 9th June at 10.30 in the morning, but I'd like to change my booking to the week after.

Dawn: What flight have you booked on?

Rebecca: QZ345.

Dawn: Sorry, what date did you say?

Rebecca: The 9th of June.

Dawn: What's your name, please?

Rebecca: Braithwaite: B-R-A-I-T-H-W-A-I-T-E.

Dawn: Ah, here you are. Braithwaite, R.

Rebecca: That's right. I'd like to change to the 16th of June if possible.

Dawn: Sorry, but all flights are full on the 16th.

Rebecca: Oh no!

Dawn: How about the 15th at 10.30 in the morning or the 17th at 9.30 in the evening?

Rebecca: Let's go for the 15th in the morning.

Dawn: You're now booked on flight QZ345 leaving at 10.30 am on the 15th of June.

Rebecca: OK.

Dawn: The fare is the same as on the flight you booked – £35. We need to charge your credit card £10 for the change. Can you give me the number, please?

Rebecca: 4223 1958 ...

Unit 14 Bright ideas

14.1 On the line

A

Jane Anderson: Jane Anderson.

Clara Rios: Hello. My name's Clara Rios. I'm a professor of chemistry at the University of Manaus in Brazil. I don't know if you remember but we met about two years ago at the Food Products Trade Fair in New York.

Jane Anderson: Yes, I remember – we talked about the market for new soft drinks in the United States. Didn't you say you were working on a new sort of drink?

Clara Rios: That's right, and you said I should get in touch when I was ready to launch it. Well, now I am ready and I'm looking for some financial backing.

Jane Anderson: OK ... You know we get hundreds of inquiries.

Clara Rios: It's not a soft drink, it's an energy drink. It contains secret ingredients from the Amazon jungle.

Jane Anderson: Really. What sort of ingredients?

Clara Rios: It's an industrial secret! I don't want to say more on the phone. If we can meet, I can tell you more about it. I'm going to be in New York next week.

Jane Anderson: Next week's going to be difficult. How about the following one?

Clara Rios: Well, I could stay over to the following Monday.

Jane Anderson:	OK ... How about Monday 25th at 2? I can see you for half an hour.
Clara Rios:	Fine. Half an hour should be enough.
Jane Anderson:	Do you know where we are? BAF Venture Capital is on Madison Avenue and 39th Street – 600 Madison Avenue. Come up to the tenth floor and ask for me at the reception desk.
Clara Rios:	OK. See you there on Monday 25th at 2pm. Thank you so much! I'm sure you won't regret it!
Jane Anderson:	My pleasure. But I can't guarantee anything.
Clara Rios:	I understand. I look forward to meeting you. Bye.
Jane Anderson:	Bye ... I hope it's good!

14.2 B

Clara Rios:	It's an industrial secret! I don't want to say more on the phone. If we can meet, I can tell you more about it. I'm going to be in New York next week.
Jane Anderson:	Next week's going to be difficult. How about the following one?
Clara Rios:	Well, I could stay over to the following Monday.
Jane Anderson:	OK ... How about Monday 25th at 2? I can see you for half an hour.
Clara Rios:	Fine. Half an hour should be enough.
Jane Anderson:	Do you know where we are? BAF Venture Capital is on Madison Avenue and 39th Street – 600 Madison Avenue. Come up to the tenth floor and ask for me at the reception desk.
Clara Rios:	OK. See you there on Monday 25th at 2pm. Thank you so much! I'm sure you won't regret it!
Jane Anderson:	My pleasure. But I can't guarantee anything.
Clara Rios:	I understand. I look forward to meeting you. Bye.
Jane Anderson:	Bye ... I hope it's good!

Unit 15 Consumer electronics

15.1 Conversation 1

Alex:	Hi, Bud. How are you?
Bud:	Fine. I had the flu' last week, but I'm OK now. And you?
Alex:	Fine, thanks.
Bud:	Have you seen the new plasma screens on the Gateway booth? They're gigantic!
Alex:	No, I must go over there and have a look. I'll go there after Bill Gates's speech – *that* should be interesting.
Bud:	I have to stay here and look after the booth.
Alex:	OK. I'll catch up with you later. Bye for now.
Bud:	Bye.

Conversation 2

Carl:	Hello, Diane.
Diane:	Oh! Hi, Carl.
Carl:	Didn't think I'd see you here. How are you?
Diane:	A bit tired. I arrived here very late last night. It was a nightmare. Had to change planes in Chicago and there was a snowstorm. We were three hours late. Anyway, I'm here now!
Carl:	So what's new this year?
Diane:	You should go to the Kodak stand – all those digital cameras. Looks like traditional photography is finished.
Carl:	Right. I'll go over there later, but I have to go back to my company's stand now.
Diane:	OK. See you later.
Carl:	See you later.

Conversation 3

Ellen:	Hey, Frank, nice to see you!
Frank:	Ellen! Good to see *you*!
Ellen:	How's your family?
Frank:	Fine, you know how it is. The kids are growing up so fast.
Ellen:	Are they into computer games?
Frank:	Yeah, they love them! I must go over to the Nintendo booth later and take a look at the latest consoles.
Ellen:	Maybe I'll see you over there later. Right now I have to go and make a phone call.
Frank:	OK. Maybe see you later.
Ellen:	See you around.

Conversation 4

Gina:	Ah, Henry, good to see you! How's business?
Henry:	Great to see you, Gina. Business is fine. DVDs are booming. Have you seen the latest DVD players? They're so cheap here in the States!
Gina:	Really!
Henry:	They're selling them in Wal-Mart for $23 each!
Gina:	You mean movies on DVD?
Henry:	No DVD *players* – $23. That means Wal-Mart must be paying the manufacturers less than $20 for them. Made in China, of course!
Gina:	Incredible.
Henry:	Incredible but true. In fact I'm having lunch with a Chinese manufacturer now. I want to see if we can get an even better deal for *our* store chain!
Gina:	Good luck!
Henry:	Thanks!

15.2 On the line

Henry Steen:	Henry Steen here.
Lee Peng:	Hello, Henry. This is Lee Peng, in Shanghai.
Henry Steen:	Hello Mr Lee. I was expecting your call. How are you?
Lee Peng:	Fine, thank you. Thanks for your e-mail. You're going ahead with your order. That's good!
Henry Steen:	Right. As I said in the e-mail, we're very interested in placing an order for DVD players, if we can get the right price.
Lee Peng:	Good! I'm sure we can come to an agreement. Do you still only want 200,000 units?
Henry Steen:	What's the unit price for 200,000?
Lee Peng:	We can supply 200,000 units over the next 12 months for 19 US dollars each.
Henry Steen:	I was hoping for a lower price.
Lee Peng:	That's the best I can do for 200,000 units. If you order more, the price will be even lower.

Unit 16 Cosmetics and pharmaceuticals

16.1

Interviewer:	Why is Avon different from other cosmetics companies?
Expert:	Well, of course, Avon products are distributed in a very interesting way, with the famous Avon representatives. This is person-to-person marketing. There are 3.9 million of these reps around the world.
Interviewer:	What's the advantage of selling in this way?
Expert:	It's a very personal form of selling. The Avon rep can visit customers and provide them with personal advice on cosmetics and other beauty products. It's what they call 'high-touch' selling.
Interviewer:	Is that their only distribution channel? Are the products distributed in other ways too?
Expert:	Yes, in some countries, Avon products are sold through shops and department stores. And in the United States, products can be bought on-line. But direct selling is the main form of distribution.
Interviewer:	I know that research and development is very important in cosmetics. Where is that done?
Expert:	Yes, it is very important. At Avon, R and D is carried out at a big research centre in New York State. A new $100 million facility on the site was opened recently.
Interviewer:	What about production?
Expert:	Some of their products are produced by outside suppliers. But most of the products are manufactured by Avon in its own plants, using raw materials from specialist companies.
Interviewer:	Right.
Expert:	For example, they built a manufacturing plant in Russia in 2003. Products made there will be sold around the world, but Russia is also going to be an important market.
Interviewer:	What other new markets are they looking at?
Expert:	They think China is going to be very important too. Direct selling can work everywhere!

16.2 On the line

Conversation 1

Receptionist:	ZRC, good morning. How may I direct your call?
A:	Hello. I'm phoning from Distripharma in Paris. We're a big European distributor of pharmaceutical products. Can I speak to someone who deals with distribution?
Receptionist:	Of course. That's Susana de Soto in marketing. Just one moment. Who may I say is calling?
A:	Suzanne Lenoir.
Receptionist:	Putting you through.
A:	Thanks.

Conversation 2

Receptionist:	ZRC, good afternoon.
B:	Hello, can I speak to someone in research and development?
Receptionist:	What's the purpose of your call?
B:	I'd like to know more about one of your R and D projects.
Receptionist:	Are you a journalist, by any chance?
B:	Actually, I am.
Receptionist:	You can talk to the press office. Just one moment.

Conversation 3

Receptionist:	ZRC, good morning.
C:	Hello. May I speak to someone in R and D?
Receptionist:	What is your call concerning?
C:	I'm a research chemist. I'm phoning about a job advertisement in the New York Times.
Receptionist:	Human resources handle all the job applications. Putting you through to HR now.
C:	Thank you.

Conversation 4

Receptionist: ZRC, good morning.

D: I'm trying to reach John Robins in R and D. I tried calling his direct line – the number's unobtainable.

Receptionist: What's the nature of your call?

D: This is his wife. Our daughter is very ill ...

Receptionist: I'll put you through right away.

Module 5 Travel and communications

Unit 17 I'm running late

17.1 On the line

Conversation 1

Alain: Allo!

Maggie: Hello Alain. Where are you?

Alain: I'm stuck in a jam on the Champs Elysées. You know, it's one of those Paris without cars days. But there are more cars than usual.

Maggie: Everyone else is here. They all came by public transport. Why didn't you?

Alain: Even if the metro was free, I wouldn't take it. I'll be there in 45 minutes. Go ahead without me!

Maggie: See you shortly.

Alain: Bye.

Conversation 2

Cathy: Hi, Mehmet. It's Cathy.

Mehmet: Cathy! Where are you?

Cathy: I'm on the ferry from Bandirma, and it's running half an hour late. We're only arriving in Istanbul now, so I'll be with you in an hour at Taksim.

Mehmet: OK.

Cathy: It'll be good to have this drink together. We have a lot to talk about!

Mehmet: We do! I'll wait for you here at the café – no problem. See you later.

Cathy: OK. Sorry about this. Bye.

Mehmet: See you shortly. Bye.

Conversation 3

Receptionist: Mega TV. Can I help you?

Anthea: Hi. My name's Anthea Johnson. I have a job interview with Tom Randall at two o'clock.

Receptionist: Uh huh.

Anthea: I've been held up. I'm stuck on a train that's broken down. They just announced we won't get to New York for another hour.

I should be there by 4. Can you tell him I've been delayed, please?

Receptionist: OK, Ms Johnson. I'll tell him.

Anthea: Thank you very much. Bye.

Receptionist: Sure. Bye.

Unit 18 Are you considerate?

18.1 On the line

Rebecca: Hello.

Helen: Hi, Rebecca. It's Helen.

Rebecca: Oh, it's you.

Helen: I tried to phone you earlier but there was no answer. Then I tried again, and the line was busy.

Rebecca: Oh, I got into work late and then I had a long call from my boss. ...

18.2

Rebecca: My journey into work was a nightmare. I don't know if I can go on with this much longer.

Helen: What happened?

Rebecca: The train was late. But there were all the other things that annoy me ...

Helen: Such as?

Rebecca: The guy opposite me was eating a hamburger. And then he got off the train and left the box on the seat with half the hamburger in it.

Helen: Urghhh! People shouldn't eat on trains and buses. It's really anti-social!

Rebecca: The guy next to me was shouting into his mobile.

Helen: Yes, I hate it when people do that.

Rebecca: And then there was a guy with a guitar playing Bob Dylan songs. He didn't know the words and he was singing out of tune. And then he went up and down the carriage asking for money.

Helen: Oh no! ... Who's Bob Dylan?

Unit 19 New ways of working

19.1 On the line

Conversation 1

Rebecca: Hello.

Mark: Hello, Rebecca. It's Mark.

Rebecca: Hi, Mark. I'm on my way to Paris. What's the latest?

Mark: There's a bit of a crisis here at the office. Carly wants all our sales reports by this evening.

Rebecca: She told us she wanted them by Monday. It's only Thursday. I'm working on mine now! I was going to e-mail it tomorrow to the company website.

Mark: She's changed her mind. Apparently the people from head office are here, and she wants to show them all the sales figures before they go.

Rebecca: I don't like being available all the time like this. It was better before mobiles …

Mark: I know what you mean.

Rebecca: The signal's very weak. I get the feeling we're going to get cut off. Bye for now.

Mark: Bye Rebecca.

Conversation 2

Rebecca: Hello.

Helen: Hi, Rebecca. It's Helen.

Rebecca: Helen, hi. I'm working on something very important. I have to finish it by this evening. And my battery's low.

Helen: OK. Give me a call at the office tomorrow morning. I've got some interesting news for you!

Rebecca: You're breaking up …

Helen: No, I'm not breaking up with my boyfriend. That's not the news …

Conversation 3

Rebecca: Hello.

Carly: Ah, Rebecca. It's Carly. How's the sales report going?

Rebecca: I'm working on it now on the train.

Carly: Will it be ready by this evening?

Rebecca: Carly, I can't hear you very well …

Carly: I said, will it be ready by this evening?

Rebecca: The train's just going into a tunnel. I'll call you later … Carly? I'm turning this thing off!

Unit 20 Why travel?

20.1

Interviewer: Professor Bremner, what are the main advantages of video-conferencing?

Paul Bremner: Well, of course, companies can save a lot of time and money when managers don't have to travel to meetings. One company I know calculated they avoided a million miles of travel in just six months, and saved two million dollars in the process!

Interviewer: But a lot of business people still travel to see colleagues and clients. Why is this, when it's so easy for people to talk to each other over video links on the internet, for example, using webcams?

Paul Bremner: There are technical reasons for this and there are also the human factors.

Interviewer: Uh huh.

Paul Bremner: Webcams are cheap, but they are not always easy to set up. Some people are good with technology, but not everyone wants to spend a lot of time getting them to work properly.

Interviewer: Right.

Paul Bremner: And they're good for one-on-one communication, but if you have a number of people in different places, you really need a video-conferencing suite.

Interviewer: OK.

Paul Bremner: The cost of these is coming down too, and the technical quality is getting very good, with big screens and so on. You just go into the room, sit down and turn on the equipment. But the conditions in the room must be exactly right, with good lighting and seating, good positioning of cameras and so on.

Interviewer: You mentioned the human factors. What are they?

Paul Bremner: People in the same organization, who know each other well, may prefer not to fly across the Atlantic for a meeting. But it can be rather formal. You need a good chairperson, and if someone wants to speak, they should put their hand up first.

Interviewer: It sounds a bit like being at school!

Paul Bremner: And if you want to show you're happy, smile broadly so the others can really see you're smiling!

Interviewer: [laughs]

Paul Bremner: But if you're meeting a client for the first time, you probably want to get on a plane and go to see them. There's nothing like a handshake and looking someone in the eye to build confidence.

20.2 On the line

Alain: Allo!

Keith: Hi, Alain. It's Keith, in London. Are you ready for our conference call?

Alain: Hi, Keith. Yes, I'm ready.

Keith: Can you hold on while I get Daljit in Bangalore?

Alain: Sure.

Keith: Hi, Daljit. It's Keith. I've got Alain in Paris on the line for our conference call.

Daljit: Good. Hi, Alain.

Alain: Hello, Daljit. How are you today?

Daljit: Fine, thanks.

Keith: Right, as I was saying at our meeting in London, the sales of *Crazy Raiders* have been fantastic. I now have the exact figures: we were aiming for $5 million profit in the second year, but we've made 8 million.

Daljit Great!

Keith: This gives us money for investment in new versions. So now, we want to develop different language versions of *Crazy Raiders* for various markets. Alain, can you say more about this?

Alain: Yes, we want to develop French, Spanish and Japanese versions. We have to decide where to develop these different versions.

Keith: Daljit, would you like to come in here?

Daljit: Well, we can't do the translation, but we can do the software development here in Bangalore for $20,000.

Alain: It would be more logical to do everything here in Paris – the translation and the software development. We can do it ...

Daljit: But it would be much more expensive.

Alain: Please let me finish! We can do it more quickly if we do it all here.

Daljit: Let's stick to my original point. How much would it cost?

Alain: We can do the translation for $20,000 and the software for 50,000.

Daljit: That's ridiculous!

Keith: Can you both calm down a moment! We haven't made any final decisions yet.

Module 6 Going global

Unit 21 Today's trends

21.1 *Miranda Rees:*

I've identified three main trends that businesses should be aware of. The first trend, of course, is 'globalisation'. It's the way the world economy works more and more as one unit. This is due to a number of factors. Capital can go around the world more or less freely for investment anywhere. Barriers to trade, for example taxes on imports, are coming down, and transport of goods is becoming cheaper. For example, the cost of shipping a container full of goods across the Pacific is just $50. And of course, telecommunications and computing costs are getting cheaper all the time. A 3-minute phone call from New York to London in 1930 cost $300 in today's money. Today it costs a dollar or less.

As a result, production of goods and services can move easily around the world. More and more manufacturing is moving to China, with its low costs and enormous workforce. And services like software programming and call centres are moving to India, with its educated English-speaking workers.

The second trend is changing populations: the way that the average age of the population of some countries is getting younger and in others is getting older. In the United States in 40 years, the average age will be 35. In some European countries, such as Italy and Germany,

it will be 55. This has important consequences for companies in the products and services that they offer, and the way that they market them. For example, advertising has until now been mainly directed at younger people. In future, seniors may be the most important group.

And the final point I want to talk about is climate change. Economic activity produces emissions of greenhouse gases, causing global warming. 'Extreme' weather is becoming more and more frequent – with extremely hot summers in many parts of the world, and more and more violent storms.

21.2 **On the line**

Naomi: Naomi Mackee.

Michael: Hi, it's Michael. Thanks for faxing over the graph.

Naomi: Sure.

Michael: Unfortunately, it's not very clear. Can I just check a few things with you on the phone? What's it about?

Naomi: The title is 'More money is not the answer.' It's about happiness in the US over the last 50 years, compared with people's income.

Michael: I see.

Naomi: The years are from 1957 in 9 year intervals – 1957, then 1966, 1975, 1984, 1993 and lastly 2002.

Michael: OK, I'm with you. And what are the figures on the vertical axis?

Naomi: They show income in thousands of dollars, starting at 0 and then 6, 12, 18 and 24 thousand dollars.

Michael: What's that dotted line on the graph that rises steadily?

Naomi: It relates to the vertical axis on the left. It shows people's income, corrected for inflation, over the last 45 or 50 years.

Michael: I follow you. So the dotted line shows income has gone up from about 9,000 to about 22,000 dollars in that time.

Naomi: That's it.

Michael: And what about the vertical axis on the right?

Naomi: That shows the percentage of people who describe themselves as very happy: it starts at zero and then you get 25, 50, 75 and 100 per cent at the top.

Michael: I get it. Wow, so the percentage of very happy people hasn't risen!

Naomi: Right. It's stayed the same.

Michael: If you look carefully, it's actually gone down from 30 per cent to about 27 per cent.

Naomi: Actually, you're right.

Michael: Thanks for your help!

Naomi: You're welcome!

Unit 22 Made in Cambodia

22.1 On the line

Martha Sanders:	Hallo.
Larry Winter:	Hi, Martha. It's Larry. How's the trip going?
Martha Sanders:	Good to hear from you!
Larry Winter:	How long have you been there now?
Martha Sanders:	I've been here three days and I've seen eight possible contractors. I've learned a lot.
Larry Winter:	Wow! You must be tired.
Martha Sanders:	Yes, but I'm getting there. There's one supplier, Phnom Penh Manufacturing – PPM – who I think is a real possibility.
Larry Winter:	Right.
Martha Sanders:	I went round their plant. PPM has the machines to produce the quantities we want – 100,000 pairs of jeans per year. I've already discussed quantities with them and they are able to produce that number. And the working conditions are very good. We've made good progress in the discussions so far.
Larry Winter:	What about the price?
Martha Sanders:	We haven't talked about price yet. I'm going back there tomorrow to see them again and talk about that. I think we can reach a deal with them.
Larry Winter:	When are you flying back to New York?
Martha Sanders:	I haven't reserved my flight yet. It all depends on what happens tomorrow!
Larry Winter:	Good luck with that! Keep me posted!
Martha Sanders:	Thanks Larry. I'll let you know how things go!
Larry Winter:	OK, bye for now!
Martha Sanders:	Bye.

22.2

Interviewer:	People buy Italian or French brands of clothing and then they see labels like 'Made in Mexico or Made in Cambodia'. What's the reason for this?
Amity Jensen:	Well of course, it's much cheaper to make things in some places than others. The cost of wages is the biggest cost in the manufacturing of clothing, and manufacturers go to places in the developing world where wages are lower. For example, in Asia, wages are typically $50 per month in Cambodia, $60 in Indonesia, $90 in the Philippines. So, clothing with international brand names is increasingly made in these places.
Interviewer:	Uh huh.
Amity Jensen:	These wages may sound very low to people in Europe or America, but living costs in these places are much lower than in Europe, and people working in clothing plants may be earning wages for the first time in their lives.
Interviewer:	What about working conditions?
Amity Jensen:	There has been a big improvement in working conditions thanks to consumers in the developed world. The big brands are very worried about their reputation. They know that it's not good for their reputation if the factories use children under 16, or if the working conditions are bad. So, they often have people whose job it is to go round and check the conditions in local contractors' factories.
Interviewer:	Mmm.
Amity Jensen:	Conditions are usually worse in the local factories that are *not* producing goods for the big brands.
Interviewer:	Right.
Amity Jensen:	And manufacturing clothing can be a first step towards economic development. Take Hong Kong. Forty years ago it was very poor, with even lower wage levels than in Cambodia or Indonesia today.
Interviewer:	Uh huh.
Amity Jensen:	Now many of the clothing manufacturers in Hong Kong have become clothing retailers, with their own designers and their own brands. They continue to manufacture clothes in Hong Kong, but also use contractors elsewhere, such as Bangladesh, Cambodia, Indonesia, Mexico, Sri Lanka, Thailand and Vietnam, and of course, mainland China itself.
Interviewer:	Right.
Amity Jensen:	Hong Kong has become a major power in the global clothing industry.
Interviewer:	I see.
Amity Jensen:	With the right planning and government action, developing countries can use low-cost manufacturing as a base from which to move on to other, more profitable activities. Low-cost manufacturing can be a first step towards economic development.

Unit 23 Tourists are everywhere

23.1 On the line

Conversation 1

Amanda:	Hello!
John Jones:	Is that Asafla Travel?

Amanda:	Yes, what do you want?
John Jones:	I've just come back from one of your holidays in the Andes – 'Mountains and jungle in Peru' was the name of the tour in the brochure.
Amanda:	Oh, yes.
John Jones:	My name's Jones, John Jones.
Amanda:	How do you spell that?
John Jones:	J-O-N-E-S. I'm phoning to complain about the conditions on the trip.
Amanda:	Can you give me your booking number from your booking confirmation?
John Jones:	There are three numbers on this letter.
Amanda:	It's in the top right hand corner.
John Jones:	Er, is this it? 937452W.
Amanda:	973 ...
John Jones:	No, 937 ...
Amanda:	937 ... What was the rest of the number?
John Jones:	452W.
Amanda:	452W. 937452W. You're not on our system.
John Jones:	But I must be!
Amanda:	Anyway, what sort of problems did you have on the trip?
John Jones:	When we stopped in the evenings, the tour leader asked me to cook – but I don't know how to cook, and anyway, when I'm on holiday I want to leave the cooking to others.
Amanda:	I'll stop you there. We don't normally deal with complaints on the phone.
John Jones:	In that case, why did you ask me about them?
Amanda:	You'll have to email our Customer Relations Department at customer dot relations at Asafla Travel – that's all one word – dot com.
John Jones:	But I don't have e-mail.
Amanda:	Well you'll have to ask a friend to use theirs, or go to an internet café or something.
John Jones:	OK, I'll do that.
Amanda:	Bye.

Conversation 2

Amanda:	Asafla Travel. Amanda speaking. How may I help you?
John Jones:	Hello. My name's Jones, John Jones. I've just come back from one of your holidays in South America – 'Mountains and jungle in Peru' was the name of the tour in the brochure. I'd like to make a complaint – well, three complaints really - and get some of my money back.
Amanda:	Jones ... Can you confirm the first line of your address?

John Jones:	32 London Road.
Amanda:	Ah, here you are. John Jones, 'Mountains and Jungle in Peru', 2nd to the 30th of June.
John Jones:	That's it.
Amanda:	What can I do for you? What exactly was the problem?
John Jones:	On the tracks in the Amazon, the truck got stuck several times and the driver wanted us to get out and push. I didn't want to do this – I was on holiday – but the driver was very rude and told me in no uncertain terms that I had to get out and push.
Amanda:	Was there anything else that caused problems?
John Jones:	When we stopped in the evenings, the tour leader asked me to cook – but I don't know how to cook, and anyway, when I'm on holiday I want to leave the cooking to others.
Amanda:	Right.
John Jones:	The climate was very difficult – in the Andes it was very cold at night, and in the Amazon it was extremely hot.
Amanda:	OK, Mr Jones. I think the best thing is if I ask our Customer Relations Manager, Samantha Trent, to give you call. When would it be convenient?
John Jones:	I'm normally here in the mornings.
Amanda:	OK, I'll ask Samantha to give you a call as soon as possible. It should be in the next couple of days.
John Jones:	OK, thank you so much.
Amanda:	Thank you. Bye.
John Jones:	Bye.

Unit 24 Eco-friendly business

24.1

Interviewer:	Can you give me some examples of the eco-friendly policies at *Boston World*?
Katherine Green:	Sure. When people think about newspapers and the environment, they think about the paper that we use. We try to use 100 per cent recycled paper.
Interviewer:	Uh huh. What other areas do your environmental policies cover?
Katherine Green:	In our offices, we try to reduce electricity and water consumption – we have automatic sensors that turn off lights when there's no one in a room, and so on.
Interviewer:	Right.
Katherine Green:	We encourage staff to reduce the amount of paper they use and to print

on both sides. We've arranged to purchase only recycled printer ink cartridges, and we tell all departments not to throw cartridges away but to send them back to the suppliers for recycling.

Interviewer: I see. What other areas have you made changes in?

Katherine Green: We encourage our employees to use public transportation to get to work, and we have facilities for people who want to cycle to work – a safe place to park their bikes, showers and so on.

Interviewer: That's good.

Katherine Green: We encourage video-conferencing by our executives, but sometimes face-to-face meetings are necessary. And of course, our journalists have to travel to meet people in order to get their stories. When our journalists and executives do travel on business, we expect them to take trains as much as possible.

Interviewer: Down to New York and Washington, for example.

Katherine Green: That's right. Of course, this isn't always possible. We calculate the number of miles of air travel that our journalists and executives do every year. Air travel is one of the main producers of carbon dioxide, one of the greenhouse gases that cause global warming.

Interviewer: Have you made any calculations on this?

Katherine Green: For example, one person on a round trip from Boston to San Francisco – about 6000 miles – produces 1.2 tonnes of carbon dioxide. We look at all the number of miles covered by our journalists and executives in a year and then pay for enough trees to be planted to take up the carbon dioxide that their journeys have produced.

Interviewer: Right.

Katherine Green: Last year our executives and journalists travelled 600,000 miles by plane, producing 120 tonnes of carbon dioxide. You need 50 trees to take up 1 tonne of carbon dioxide, so last year we planted 6,000 trees, to take up those 120 tonnes of carbon dioxide that those flights produced.

Interviewer: Wow! Where were these trees planted?

Katherine Green: We gave money to environmental organisations to plant trees all over the world – North and South America, Europe and Asia, you name it ...

24.2 On the line

Caller 1

Caller 1: If I can just check a couple of figures. You spent nearly $2 million on electricity in your offices last year.

PR officer: Yes. One point nine million to be exact.

Caller 1: And the number of miles flown by your staff in the last year was 500,000?

PR officer: That's right – 500,000 miles.

Caller 2

Caller 2: So you use 100 per cent recycled paper in your printing plant?

PR officer: Unfortunately, that's technically not possible. For example, we can't use recycled paper for our magazine sections.

Caller 2: So what is the correct figure?

PR officer: It's more like 84 per cent.

Caller 3

PR officer: Right. There's a lot to discuss.

Caller 3: Yes, why don't we meet up for lunch or coffee?

PR officer: How about coffee on Friday morning? Starbucks, in Main Street?

Caller 3: Sounds great. Would 11 o'clock suit you?

PR officer: Fine.

Answer key

1 World of work

Grammar **A** What are you doing?   I'm (I am) writing an e-mail.

What's (What is) she doing?   She's (She is) having lunch with a colleague.

What are they doing?   They're (They are) driving home.

B 1 Where's Pilar going right now? – She's taking the subway to work.

2 Who's Sonia talking to right now? – She's talking to a group of tourists.

3 What's he doing right now? – He's taking a break and drinking tea.

4 What's he watching on television right now? – He's watching an old James Bond film.

Speaking **A** 1 Rio 8 am   3 Sydney 9 pm   5 Kyoto 8 pm

2 New York 7 am   4 Paris 1 pm   6 Kuwait 2 pm

B 1b   2c   3a

ON THE LINE **A** a 3   b 1   c 3   d 2   e 4   f 1   g 2   h 4

2 I spend all my time in meetings

Grammar **A** Do you use a PDA?   Yes, I do. / No, I don't.

Why do you use a PDA?   Because I can check my email when I'm out of the office.

Does Daljit use a PDA?   Yes, she does. / No, she doesn't.

Why doesn't she use a PDA?   Because she prefers using her laptop and mobile phone.

Vocabulary and listening **A** 1 organised, get on well with people, tidy, nice

2 punctual, good with computers, efficient, good with detail, polite

B 1 rude, in a bad mood, untidy, complete mess, disorganised

2 hopeless with computers, late, inefficient

ON THE LINE **A** a 3   b 1   c 2

B a 3 Maybe it's easier if I send you an e-mail.

b 2 Could I call you later?

c 1 Can I call you back later?

3 We're behind schedule

Listening **A**

Stages	Year 1							Year 2									
	J	J	A	S	O	N	D	J	F	M	A	M	J	J	A	S	O
Finalise game design	✔	✔	✔														
Recruit developers		✔	✔														
Write software				✔	✔	✔	✔	✔	✔	✔	✔						
Design packaging								✔	✔	✔	✔	✔					
Manufacture product												✔	✔	✔	✔	✔	✔
Launch product																✔	

Grammar

A

Regular verbs	Irregular verbs
finalise – finalised	find – found
need – needed	go – went
recruit – recruited	write – wrote

Reading and speaking

A For various reasons, the project is behind schedule. The game design stage <u>went</u> OK and they <u>finalised</u> it ahead of schedule, at the end of July last year.

Our problems <u>started</u> just after that. We <u>needed</u> to recruit 50 developers, but at first we only <u>found</u> 20 – last July there <u>were</u> so many other companies who <u>wanted</u> to recruit the same people. We only <u>finished</u> recruitment in December last year. So the software writing stage <u>started</u> two months late, and only <u>finished</u> last month.

The packaging designers <u>started</u> work on schedule, but we <u>didn't like</u> their work. We <u>looked</u> for another design company, and what they <u>did</u> was very good, but we <u>lost</u> a month and the work only <u>ended</u> in July.

There <u>were</u> technical problems at the factory and manufacturing is starting three months late, in August. We can still launch the product in September, but with lower stocks of finished video games than we planned. Another problem is that we are over budget by 20 per cent!

B

	Year 1							Year 2									
Stages	J	J	A	S	O	N	D	J	F	M	A	M	J	J	A	S	O
Finalise game design	✔	✔															
Recruit developers		✔	✔	✔	✔	✔	✔										
Write software						✔	✔	✔	✔	✔	✔	✔					
Design packaging								✔	✔	✔	✔	✔	✔				
Manufacture product															✔	✔	✔
Launch product																✔	

C
1 If you finish a project ahead of schedule, you finish it early.
2 If you finish a project on schedule, you finish it on time.
3 If you finish a project behind schedule, you finish it late.
4 If you finish a project under budget, it costs less than you planned.
5 If you finish a project on budget, it costs exactly what you planned.
6 If you finish a project over budget, it costs more than you planned.

ON THE LINE

A
1 I'm rather worried about the delays.
2 I didn't want to bother you.
3 The schedule's very tight.
4 If customers come into the shops and can't buy the product, it's a disaster!
5 Yes, but they're charging us more because of the rush.
6 Yes, but don't panic! The project is going to be a big success.

C

Budget (US$)	Planned	Actual
Design game	300,000	450,000
Write software	750,000	1,500,000
Design packaging	7,000	10,000
Manufacture product	92,000	133,000
TOTAL	1,149,000	2,093,000

4 Are you a team player?

Grammar **A** 1 He prefers working with others to working on his own.

2 I hate eating on my own in restaurants.

3 They dislike being in the same room together.

4 I enjoy driving to work – it gives me time to be by myself and to think.

5 We should finish testing the software before giving it to users.

6 She's terrible at keeping records of what she does.

7 He's bad at telling other people what's happening.

ON THE LINE **A** a 2   b 3   c 4   d 1

B 1b   2a   3a   4a

Writing   **Model answer**

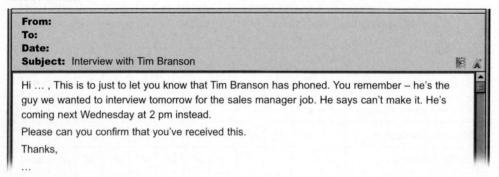

Grammar review and development 1–4

present simple: *do/does*

A | 1 sell | 7 believe |
|---|---|
| 2 make | 8 give |
| 3 want | 9 train |
| 4 offers | 10 offer |
| 5 employ | 11 have |
| 6 hope | |

present simple: adverbs

B 1 **Q:** Do you always sell your programmes abroad?
   A: … We don't always sell them abroad.

2 **Q:** Does the company often fire staff?
   A: We don't often fire people … we don't often make mistakes in our recruitment.

3 **Q:** Do you usually talk to programme makers about ideas for new programmes?
   A: We always discuss new programmes with them.

4 **Q:** Do you and the programme makers sometimes argue?
   A: We sometimes disagree about ideas for programmes.

5 **Q:** Does the company often win prizes for its programmes?
   A: Of course! We never have a year without prizes.

present continuous: activity in progress

A 1 Who is Giorgio seeing? – b

2 What are they talking about? – d

3 Where are they meeting? – e

4 Why are they meeting there? – a

5 What are they doing? – c

present continuous: temporary situations

B 1 Anita is on a training course, so I'm using her office – it's better than mine.

2 There's a train strike, so everyone's driving to work – the traffic is terrible and people are arriving very late.

3 What's more, a lot of people are off sick, so we are doing less work and customers are complaining.

4 In addition, my computer isn't working, so I'm not sending any e-mails.

5 And, above all, the company is reorganising, so everyone is feeling very worried.

past simple

A 1 They wanted to manufacture 500,000 games before the launch. Did they actually manufacture 500,000?
– No, they didn't. In the end, they only made 250,000.

2 They wanted to start writing Version 2 of Crazy Raiders at the end of first year. Did they actually start writing it then?
– No they didn't. In the end, they only started at the end of Year 3.

3 They wanted to develop business with a partner in London. Did they actually do this in the end?
– No they didn't. In the end, they found a new partner in Amsterdam.

4 They wanted to make $5 million profit in the second year. Did they actually make $5 million profit?
– No, they didn't. In the end, they made $7 million.

5 They wanted to write the software for two new games. Did they actually do this in the end?
– No, they didn't. In the end, they wrote the software for four new games.

5 Staying in

Listening and vocabulary

A **Speaker 1:** picture on the right.
Speaker 2: picture on the left.

B
armchairs 1 noun	**clean** 2 adj	**comfortable** 1 adj	**cosy** 1 adj
elegant 2 adj	**equipment** 2 noun	**flowery** 2 adj	**furniture** 2 noun
heavy 1 adj	**hi-tech** 2 adj	**minimalist** 2 adj	**modern** 2 adj
screen 2 noun	**thick** 1 adj	**television** 1 noun	**traditional** 1 adj
typical 2 adj	**ugly** 1 adj	**wooden** 1 adj	

Grammar

count and uncount nouns

A Some nouns can have a plural form. They are count nouns.

Other nouns do not have a plural form. You cannot use them with *a/an*. They are uncount nouns.

Some nouns can be both count and uncount.

B 1 money 4 information, knowledge
2 traffic 5 equipment
3 advice 6 employment

ON THE LINE **A** **Emma:** You're through to the order department. My name's Emma. How can I help?
Martin: I have your catalogue in front of me. I'd like to order some Avgard furniture.

B stock 3 system 2 available 1 guaranteed 5 deliver 4

C **Emma:** Order department. Emma speaking. What can I do for you?
Martin: Hello. I ordered some Avgard furniture from you last week. Was it you I spoke to?

D exchange 3 defect 2 refund 1 credit note 4

6 Museums and exhibitions

1 traditional – done in a way that it has always been done – b

2 successful – having the wanted result – c

3 marketable – able to be sold – g

4 commercial – related to business – e

5 acceptable – good enough for a particular purpose – d

6 popular – liked by a lot of people – a

7 aggressive – using strong methods that some people do not like – f

A You use the present perfect to talk about the past without mentioning a specific time.

You use the past simple when you mention a specific time.

B MUSEUMS <u>have</u> never <u>had</u> it so good. New ones are being built all over the place, and existing ones are getting bigger; money-raising campaigns <u>have</u> never <u>been</u> so successful, and visitor numbers <u>have</u> never <u>been</u> higher: American museums now attract more than a billion visitors a year.

As they <u>have become</u> more marketable, some museums <u>have begun</u> to behave in more commercial ways. And it's working. Tate Modern in London and the Guggenheim Museum in New York, two of the most commercial big museums, are doing particularly well.

This <u>has forced</u> the directors of all museums to ask: How far can the commercialisation of an art museum go? Which marketing techniques are acceptable, and which are not? Will there in future be two kinds of museum: the temples of high culture, and the more popular entertainment centres?

The controversy is over the marketing methods of the Guggenheim Museum. Its methods are aggressive, even by New York standards. Three years ago, the museum <u>put on</u> an exhibition of motorcycles sponsored by BMW, a German car maker. But it <u>was</u> an exhibition last autumn of dresses by Giorgio Armani, an Italian fashion designer, that really <u>annoyed</u> people. The exhibition <u>was sponsored</u> by *In Style*, a fashion magazine, but Mr Armani <u>has given</u> $15m to the museum. Some critics <u>have called</u> this 'rent'. ['When merchants enter the temple', *adapted from The Economist, 19 Apr 2001*]

A Availability: 3 weeks from now

Booking made for: Saturday March 30th at 7.00 pm

Must arrive by: 7.30 and can stay until 11.00

3 adults @ $10 = $30

1 child @ $6 = $6

Total = $36

7 Family entertainment

	Where from?	liked:	criticised:	because:
Visitor 1	Paris	the Rodeo	the Mexican restaurant	there was no wine
Visitor 2	Bangalore	Delhi restaurant; cowboy cooking demonstrations	the roller coaster	there were long lines
Visitor 3	Liverpool	western country music	the Big Steak restaurant	there were no vegetarian options

1 comfortable +   3 unattractive –   5 clean +   7 boring –

2 terrifying –   4 exciting +   6 dangerous –   8 professional +

ON THE LINE **A**

	Satisfaction score	No. of visitors last year
Farwest, Utah	7.28	500,000
Shark Paradise, Miami	9.26	2,250,000
Mountain Village, Japan	8.99	1,500,000
Future City, France	7.50	750,000
Kings and Queens, UK	8.16	1,250,000

B Just a moment, 5   Maybe. 6   Yes, but... 3

Before you go on, ... 1   I wouldn't say that. 2   Let me just finish... 4

Writing **A** **Model answer**

MEMO

From: Taro Suzuki

To: all TS Leisure theme park directors

Thank you for coming to Kyoto last week for a very useful meeting. I hope you all had a pleasant trip back home.

I have thought long and hard about investment in the group's theme parks. All your presentations were excellent, but I have decided to invest the whole budget in the chair lift scheme at our Mountain Village park here in Japan. The director of the park gave a particularly good presentation and persuaded me that this was the right investment.
I'm sorry that the other parks will not receive investment this year, but I look forward to meeting you all again next year to discuss next year's investment plans.

8 Leisure in 2050

Grammar **A** You use *will* to say that something in the future is quite certain.

You use *might, may* or *could* to say that it is probable, but not certain, that something will happen in the future.

B **Model answers.** *(Discuss the other possibilities with your teacher.)*

1 In 2050, China might be the world's biggest economy.

2 London, Paris and New York may still be the most important world cities for business and the arts.

3 English might still be the main language of international communication.

4 Roads may be less crowded – there may be much less commuting. Cars may just be for leisure use in the country and between cities.

5 Climate change, with increased temperatures, means that skiing might no longer be possible in Europe in resorts below 3000 metres.

6 Climate change also means that northern Europe might have a more Mediterranean-type climate. Countries like Sweden and Denmark might produce wine!

Vocabulary **A** 1 futurology   5 predictions

2 crystal ball   6 strategy

3 trends   7 objectives

4 forecasts

ON THE LINE **A** OK. 2   Right. 3   Aha... 5

Yes. 1   And what about... 4   Really! 6

B

TS leisure	Now	In 10 years
Theme parks	6	9
TS Leisure Clubs	10	7–8
TS Leisure Senior Clubs	1	7
Films with actors	3	1–2
Animated films	5	20

Grammar review and development 5–8

count and uncount nouns

A 1c 2g 3e 4b 5f 6d 7a

B

A	B
1 Do you do a lot of reading?	No, I don't do a lot of reading. / No, I don't do much reading.
2 Do you do a lot of shopping?	No, I don't do a lot of shopping. / No, I don't do much shopping.
3 Do you do a lot of cooking?	Yes, I do a lot of cooking.
4 Do you do a lot of entertaining?	We do a lot of entertaining.
5 Do you do a lot of gardening?	No, I don't do a lot of gardening. / No, I don't do much gardening.

Present perfect and past simple

A
1 did, start   7 developed   13 have fallen
2 started   8 stopped   14 have made
3 was   9 were   15 bought
4 did, grow   10 was   16 have tried
5 grew   11 Have, been   17 have, succeeded
6 opened   12 have, been

Will and *may, might, could*

A 1b 2c 3a 4d 5e

9 Getting fit

Reading **B** 1 T   2 F   3 F   4 F   5 T   6 T

ON THE LINE **A**

	Dynamo	Elan	Fun
Normal joining fee	S$800	S$500	S$450
Normal annual fee	S$3000	S$3500	S$2000
Corporate discount offered	30 per cent	25 per cent	10 per cent
Minimum number of memberships to obtain discount	50	30	40
Other facilities	café, supermarket	café, supermarket, doctor	–

B a 3 b 1 c 1 d 3 e 2 f 1

Grammar

Your gym is cheaper than the others.
Dynamo has the best facilities.

A Complete the table.

	comparative	**superlative**
one syllable *fit low*	Add -er: *fitter lower*	add –est: *fittest lowest*
two or more syllables: *expensive, convenient*	use 'more': *more expensive more convenient*	use 'most': *most expensive most convenient*
irregular *good bad*	*better worse*	*best worst*

C 1 The fees at the Algarve are expensive, but the fees at the Bellevue are even more expensive.

2 The facilities at the Algarve are good, but the facilities at the Bellevue are even better.

3 The course at the Algarve is difficult, but the course at the Bellevue is even more difficult.

4 The waiting list at the Algarve is long, but the waiting list at the Bellevue is even longer.

5 The members at the Algarve are rich, but the members at the Bellevue are even richer.

6 The clubhouse at the Algarve is beautiful, but the clubhouse at the Bellevue is even more beautiful.

7 The food in the restaurant at the Algarve is delicious, but the food at the Bellevue is even more delicious.

10 Asleep on the job?

Reading **B** 1 She's a novelist.

2 She works from 5 till lunchtime.

3 He feels tired and stressed.

4 He feels fine.

5 No, she doesn't.

6 She feels exhausted and very sleepy.

ON THE LINE **A** and **B**

How many hours a week do you work?	37
Do you do shift work?	No, I work normal office hours.
When do feel at your best during the day?	After lunch.
When do you feel at your worst?	About an hour after I get to work.
How long do you take for lunch?	An hour.
What do you do for lunch?	I go to a gym, and then I have a light lunch at the café there.
Do you drink wine or beer with lunch?	No, because if I do, I feel sleepy in the afternoon.
How much tea and coffee do you drink during the day?	I never drink tea. I don't like it. I have two cups of coffee for breakfast, two more when I get to work, and a coffee after lunch.

Writing 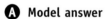 **Ⓐ Model answer**

REPORT

 AR SURVEYS

Subject: Tiredness at work

This report presents the findings of our recent research into tiredness at work.

We found that most people (58 per cent) work between 31 and 40 hours a week. Only 8 per cent of people work in shifts. Most people feel at their best in the morning (36 per cent) and at their worst in the afternoon (45 per cent). 57 per cent of people take between 45 and 75 minutes for lunch. 45 per cent of people go to a cafe or restaurant for lunch, but only 12 per cent drink wine or beer with their food. Consumption of tea and coffee is mainly between 1 and 3 cups per day (55 per cent), with 41 per cent altogether drinking four cups or more. Only 4 per cent of people drink no tea or coffee at all.

---

11 Dealing with stress

Reading and listening Ⓐ Employees shouldn't:

1 rely on caffeine or aspirin

2 drink alcohol to reduce stress

3 eat too much or eat badly.

The bank provides:

4 special relaxation areas at the bank, where people can relax and even take a nap or play table football

5 free health club membership

6 art and music classes.

Grammar Ⓐ

You	must	work harder.
	should	relax more.

You	mustn't (must not)	smoke so much.
	should't (should not)	work so hard.

Ⓑ 1 They shouldn't smoke so much.

2 They mustn't be so lazy.

3 They shouldn't work so hard.

4 They shouldn't drink so much coffee.

5 They mustn't watch so much television.

6 They mustn't eat so many hamburgers.

N THE LINE Ⓐ 1 T 2 F 3 F 4 T 5 F

---

12 Work-life balance

Reading and writing Ⓑ

1 giving	6 find
2 about	7 for
3 on	8 at
4 like	9 look
5 for	10 best

Grammar

A With the present perfect, you use

for with a period of time

since with a point in time

B 1 How long have you lived in Vancouver? - For ten years.

2 How long have you been a web designer? – Since 1998.

3 How long have you worked for JPG? – For three years.

4 How long have you had your present job? – For 15 months.

5 How long have you studied French? – Since last September.

6 How long have you been a member of the Vancouver French Film Club? – For six months.

Grammar review and development 9–12

Comparatives and superlatives

B Model answers

1 Production was much lower in August because of the annual holiday.

2 Production reached its lowest point in September.

3 Production was higher in November than in December because of the Christmas holidays.

must and *should*

A Model answers

1 We should call an ambulance. We shouldn't move the person. We should cover them so they are warm.

2 We must tell customers to bring the product back for a free repair. We shouldn't fire the mechanics. We should say, 'These things happen. Can you bring back your car next week?'

3 We must tell the employee that we know about their activities. We should call the police. We shouldn't accuse the employee before we are sure of the facts.

4 We should improve the parts ordering system. We shouldn't deny that there is a problem with the servicing. We must fire the people in the parts department.

5 We shouldn't think that the company's money problems will just go away. We must analyse why there are losses. We should control costs.

B Model answers

1 Should I call an ambulance?

2 Should I tell customers to bring back the product for a free repair?

3 Should I call the police?

4 Should I fire the people in the parts department?

5 Should I try to control costs?

present perfect with *for* and *since*

A **For:** 2, 4, 6

Since: 1, 3, 5, 7, 8

B 1 The Swedish company Stora has existed for over 700 years. It was founded in the 13th century.

2 Thomas Watson started IBM in 1924. It has made electronic computers since 1953.

3 Warren Buffet, the world's greatest investor, has managed Berkshire Hathaway since he left school.

4 General Motors has been the world's biggest car company for nearly 40 years.

5 People have bought and sold insurance at Lloyds of London since the middle of the seventeenth century.

6 Women have worn Chanel no. 5 for decades: it never goes out of fashion.

13 Low-cost airlines

Vocabulary **A** a3 b4 c2 d1

B

Traveller	Place coming from	Reason for trip	Fare paid	Satisfaction level*
University teacher	Nice	See contacts on a research project	£70 return	6
Retired man	Barcelona	In UK to see lawyers	£95	5
Bank executive	Geneva	See director of another bank	£84	4
Supermarket worker	Prague	Holiday with girlfriend	£63	7

Grammar **A** You use the past simple with *ago* to talk about past events.

You put *ago* after a period of time.

This happened five years ago.

B 1 How long ago did the Superbrand Council recognise easyJet as 'an outstanding brand name'?

2 How long ago did Independent Television show its first series about easyJet?

3 How long ago did the London Stock Exchange list easyJet shares for the first time?

4 Sir Colin Chandler took over as chairman four years ago.

5 EasyJet ordered 120 aircraft from Airbus three years ago.

6 The first Airbus A319 went into service two years ago.

14 Bright ideas

Reading **B** a2 b3 c1

Grammar **A** You use the past continuous to talk about something that was in progress when something else happened.

You form the past continuous with *was/were* and the *-ing* form of the verb.

B 1 I was going home on the train when it stopped in a tunnel.

2 We sere eating at a restaurant when the lights went out.

3 I was watching a film at a cinema when the screen went black.

4 I was taking a lift when it suddenly got stuck between floors.

5 We were listening to music on a battery radio at home when they interrupted the programme.

6 I was having beer in a bar when everything went dark and everyone cheered.

ON THE LINE **A** 1 She's a professor of chemistry.

2 A new sort of drink.

3 She's looking for finance to launch the drink.

4 Yes, she has.

5 Monday 25th at 2 o'clock.

B **Clara:** If we can meet, I can tell you more about it. I'm going to be in New York next week.

Jane: Next week's going to be difficult. How about the following one?

Clara: Well, I could stay over to the following Monday.

Jane: OK... How about Monday 25th at 2? I can see you for half an hour.

Clara: Fine. Half an hour should be enough.

Jane: Do you know where we are? BAF Venture Capital is on Madison Avenue and 39th street – 600 Madison Avenue. Come up to the tenth floor and ask for me at reception.

Clara: OK. See you there on Monday 25th at 2pm. Thank you so much! I'm sure you won't regret it!

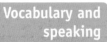

Vocabulary and speaking

A
1 ingredients
2 industrial secret
3 manufacturing
4 plant
5 marketing
6 consumers
7 start-up capital
8 investors
9 business plan

15 Consumer electronics

Reading and vocabulary

B a5, 6 b1, 7 c3 d4 e2, 8, 9, 10

C 1b 2c 3c 4d 5b 6a 7d 8a

Listening and speaking

A
a 'small talk'	b the product they talk about	c what they are going to do next
travel to Las Vegas 2	plasma screens 1	make a phone call 3
health 1	games consoles 3	go back to company's stand 2
work 4	DVD players 4	have lunch with a supplier 4
family 3	digital cameras 2	listen to Bill Gates's speech 1

B
1 **A:** Hi, Bud, how are you?
  B: Fine. I had flu last week, but I'm OK now. And you?
  A: Fine, thanks.

2 **C:** Hello, Diane.
  D: Oh, hi, Carl.
  C: Didn't think I'd see you here. How are you?
  D: A bit tired. I arrived here very late last night. It was a nightmare. Had to change planes in Chicago and there was a snowstorm. We were three hours late. Anyway, I'm here now!

3 **E:** Hey, Frank, nice to see you!
  F: Good to see *you*, Ellen.
  E: How's your family?
  F: Fine, you know how it is. The kids are growing up so fast.

4 **G:** Ah, Henry, good to see you! How's business?
  H: Great to see you, Gina. Business is fine. DVDs are booming. Have you seen the latest DVD players. They're so cheap here in the States!

Grammar

A
1 If you order 300,000 units, we'll reduce the unit price to $17.
2 If we deliver 400,000 over 3 years, the price will be even lower.
3 If I give you a lower price, I'll lose money.
4 If we reach an agreement today, my personal assistant will fax the contract this evening.
5 If you come to Shanghai, I'll show you all the sights.
6 If you go to a competitor, I won't be happy.

ON THE LINE

A Quantity: 200,000 units   Delivery period: 12 months   Unit price: $19 each

Model answer

Dear Mr Lee,

It was good to talk to you today. This is to confirm that we wish to order 400,000 units over the next three years at a cost of $17 per unit. We agreed on the following payment terms: you will invoice us every three months for the DVD players delivered in that period. I am sending a contract with these details to you by courier today.

Yours sincerely,

Henry Steen

16 Cosmetics and pharmaceuticals

Vocabulary and listening

A 1b 2a 3f 4g 5c 6e 7d

B 2, 1, 5, 4, 7, 6, 3

⦿N THE LINE

A a 2 b 1 c 4 d 3

B a1 b1 c2 d1 e4 f4 g3 h 3

Grammar

A 1 Its products are sold in department stores.

2 Its products are marketed all over the world.

3 Its products are manufactured in its own plants.

4 Its Russian manufacturing plant was built in 2003.

5 Its new research centre in New York state was opened in 2004.

Grammar review and development 13–16

past simple with *ago*

A Model answers

1 When did Ryanair start its Dublin-London route? - Nearly 20 years ago.

2 When did Ryanair list its shares on the Dublin stock exchange? – Nine years ago.

3 When did Ryanair order 45 planes from Boeing? – Seven years ago.

4 When did Ryanair launch its website? – Five years ago.

5 When did Ryanair open Frankfurt-Hahn as its second European base? – Three years ago.

6 When did Ryanair take over the Buzz airline from KLM? – Two years ago.

B 1 How long ago did Ryanair start on the Dublin-London route?

2 How long ago did Ryanair list its shares on the Dublin stock exchange?

3 How long ago did Ryanair order 45 planes from Boeing?

4 How long ago did Ryanair launch its website?

5 How long ago did Ryanair open Frankfurt-Hahn as its second European base?

6 How long ago did Ryanair take over Buzz airline from KLM?

past continuous

A 1 I was writing the business plan when my computer crashed and I lost 50 pages.

2 I was going to see a venture capital company when I heard it was bankrupt.

3 We were preparing to launch the product when there was a fire in the factory.

4 Sales were rising fast when our sales manager left the company.

5 We were getting into the Asian market when there was a financial crash there.

6 I was talking to a possible client when I found out they had already signed with a competitor.

first conditional

A 1b 2e 3f 4c 5d 6a

B 3 Unless you deliver on time in the future, we won't order from you again.

4 Unless you make your machinery safe, we'll close your factory.

5 Unless you tell us exactly what you want, we can't let you have it.

6 Unless you correct the information in your advertisements, we'll investigate further.

passive

A 1 Gold is mined by DeBeers in South Africa.

2 The ore is transformed into pure gold by refiners.

3 The gold is sold on international markets.

4 Gold is bought by jewellers.

5 The gold is turned by specialist workers into jewellery.

6 The most expensive jewellery is sold by retailers in streets such as Bond Street in London.

7 Jewellery is bought by rich and not-so-rich people.

B 1 Who is gold mined by?

2 Who is the ore transformed by?

3 Who is the gold sold by?

4 Who is gold bought by?

5 Who is the gold turned into jewellery by?

6 Who is the most expensive jewellery sold by?

7 Who is jewellery bought by?

17 I'm running late

Reading and vocabulary

B 1f   2b, d, e, g   3h   4c

C 1f   2h   3g   4b   5e   6d   7c   8a

Grammar

A Questions with Model answers

1 If public transport was free, would you use it more? – No, I'd still use my car.

2 If car tax doubled, would you sell your car? – No, I'd keep it even if car tax tripled.

3 If your journey to work took more than two hours, would you move nearer to work? – Yes, I would move to somewhere nearer.

4 If you had to pay to drive into the city centre, would you use public transport? – No, I'd pay up to €15 a day to drive into the centre.

ON THE LINE A

	City	Reason for journey	Problem
1	Paris	meeting	stuck in traffic
2	Istanbul	drink at a café	ferry running late
3	New York	job interview	train broken down

B It's running half an hour late. 2   I'm stuck in a jam. 1   Go ahead without me. 1

I've been held up. 3   I'll be with you in an hour. 2   Can you tell him I've been delayed, please? 3

18 Are you considerate?

Grammar

A Model sentences

1 People should wait for passengers to get off before they get onto trains.
People shouldn't get onto trains before passengers have time to get off.

2 People shouldn't shout into their mobile phones.

3 People should put their feet on the floor.
People shouldn't put their feet on the seat opposite them.

4 People shouldn't eat smelly food.

5 People shouldn't use loud personal stereos.
They should turn their stereos down.

6 People shouldn't drop litter.

B 1c   2a   3b   4e   5f   6d

ⓒN THE LINE **Ⓐ** 1 and 2

Ⓑ a4   b2   c8

Vocabulary and speaking

Ⓐ 1b   2a   3e   4c   5d

Ⓒ

noun	adjective	adverb
courtesy	courteous	courteously
aggression	aggressive	aggressively
consideration	considerate	considerately

19 New ways of working

Reading and vocabulary

Ⓑ 1b   2c   3a   4e   5f   6d

ⓒN THE LINE **Ⓐ** a3   b1   c2   d1   e3   f2

20 Why travel?

Listening and speaking

Ⓐ 1 Companies can save a lot of time and money when managers don't have to travel to meetings.

2 There are technical reasons and there are also the human factors.

3 They are cheap but they are not always easy to set up. They are good for one-to-one communication, but if you have a number of people in different places, you really need a video-conferencing suite.

4 The cost is coming down, and the technical quality is getting very good. You just go into the room, sit down and turn on the equipment. But the conditions in the room must be exactly right.

5 Meetings can be rather formal. You need a good chairperson, and if someone wants to speak, they should put their hand up first.

Grammar **Ⓐ** 1c   2b   3a   4d   5e

ⓒN THE LINE **Ⓐ** 1 Can you hold on while I get Daljit in Bangalore?

2 I've got Alain in Paris on the line for our conference call.

3 Right, as I was saying at our meeting in London, ...

4 Alain, can you say more about this?

5 Daljit, would you like to come in here?

6 Can you both calm down a moment!

Writing **Model answer**

Ⓐ

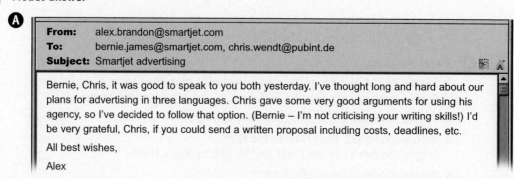

From:	alex.brandon@smartjet.com
To:	bernie.james@smartjet.com, chris.wendt@pubint.de
Subject:	Smartjet advertising

Bernie, Chris, it was good to speak to you both yesterday. I've thought long and hard about our plans for advertising in three languages. Chris gave some very good arguments for using his agency, so I've decided to follow that option. (Bernie – I'm not criticising your writing skills!) I'd be very grateful, Chris, if you could send a written proposal including costs, deadlines, etc.

All best wishes,

Alex

Grammar review and development 17–20

Second conditional

Ⓐ Questions with model answers

1 Would you raise the minimum wage?
– I wouldn't raise the minimum wage. It's already too high for a lot of companies.

2 Would you reduce the number of working hours per week?
– I wouldn't reduce the number of working hours. It wouldn't be good for the economy.

3 Would you increase the number of weeks of paid holiday?
- I wouldn't do this, as companies would have to pay, and they can't afford it.

4 Would you increase the length of parental leave when people have children?
– I would increase the length of parental leave. At the moment, leave is not long enough.

5 Would you force companies to have crèches for employees with children?
– I wouldn't do this. Crèches should be set up independently of companies by other organisations.

6 Would you subsidise broadband internet access so more people could work from home?
– I would do this, because encouraging more people to work from home would help solve our traffic problems.

Ⓒ Model answers

1 I'd live in a big house in the country, miles from the nearest village.

2 I wouldn't work from home, because I like seeing my colleagues every day.

3 I'd build a garage, so I wouldn't have to park in the street.

4 I'd stop using e-mail.

5 I'd spend the money on buying new furniture.

should/shouldn't

Ⓐ Model answers

1 You should learn the language. Not everyone can speak English.

2 No, you needn't shake hands with everyone.

3 Yes, you should invite colleagues out to lunch if you want to learn what's happening in the organisation.

4 You should take flowers, chocolate, or wine.

5 You should say *Hej!*

6 You shouldn't talk about politics or religion.

7 You should say *Tack för ikväll.*

8 You should phone to thank the person within a week or so.

Verbs with prepositions and particles

Ⓐ 1d 2a 3c 4b

Ⓑ **1** held up

2 broken down

3 breaking up

4 Calm down!

5 coming down

21 Today's trends

Listening and speaking

Ⓐ **1** globalisation   **2** changing populations   **3** climate change

Ⓑ

For example	For instance	As a result	As a consequence	This has important consequences
Due to	The first trend	The second trend	The final point	First(ly) Second(ly) Third(ly)

C **Trend 1:** Globalisation due to
- free movement of capital around the world for investment
- barriers to trade coming down
- cheaper transport of goods
- cheaper telecommunications and computing costs.

As a result, production of goods and services can move easily around the world, for example, to China for manufacturing, and to India for many services like call centres and software programming.

Trend 2: Changing populations. For example, in 40 years,
- in some European countries, the average age will be 55
- in the United States, it will be 35.

This has important consequences for companies: the products and services that they offer and the way that they market them. Advertising will be less directed to younger people and more to seniors.

Trend 3: Climate change. Extreme weather is becoming more frequent, for example, violent storms and extremely hot summers.

Grammar

A You use the present continuous to talk about trends happening now.

B 1 People are living longer, healthier lives.
2 Company employees are working longer hours each day.
3 Unemployment is falling.
4 More and more young people are going to university.
5 House prices are rising very fast in some countries.
6 Traffic in cities is moving more and more slowly.

ON THE LINE

A

| I see. | OK, I'm with you. | I follow you. | That's it. |
| I get it. | Right. | I understand. | That's correct. |

rise	level off	stay the same: *It's*	go down: *It's actually gone*
go up: *It has gone up.*		*stayed the same.*	*down from 30 per cent to*
increase			*about 27 per cent.*
			come down
			decrease
			fall

C

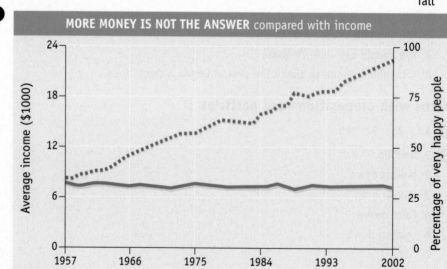

Writing

Model answer

The graph compares income in the US since 1957 with percentages of people who say they are very happy. In 1957, average income was about $9000, and about 30 per cent of people said they were very happy. Between 1957 and 2002, average income rose to about $22,000, but the percentage of people who say they are very happy fell slightly, from about 35 per cent to 30 per cent. This shows that rising income has not meant increased happiness!

22 Made in Cambodia

Reading and vocabulary

A 1c 2e 3f 4a 5d 6b

ON THE LINE **A** a2 b1 c5 d7 e6 f4 g3

Grammar

A You use the present perfect (negative) with *yet* to say that something has not happened.

B 1 I've already packed my bags, but I haven't phoned for a taxi yet.
2 I've already arrived at the airport, but I haven't got on the plane yet.
3 I've already landed in Phnom Penh, but I haven't picked up my baggage yet.
4 I've already got to the hotel, but I haven't had dinner yet.
5 I've already seen four contractors, but I haven't chosen one yet.
6 I've already decided the price, but I haven't signed the contract yet.

Listening

A manufacturing, contractors, developing world, plant

B 1T 2T 3T 4F 5F 6T 7F 8F

23 Tourists are everywhere

Vocabulary

A 1 satisfied   4 disappointed
2 delighted   5 complaints
3 dissatisfied   6 word-of-mouth

Grammar

B 1 He asked us to put up the tents.
2 He told us to clean the truck.
3 He wanted us to drive all night.
4 He told us not to complain about the climate.
5 He advised us to speak to the customer relations manager.

ON THE LINE **A** 1 2
2 1, 3, 4

24 Eco-friendly business

Listening and vocabulary

A 1 For the newspaper, use paper that is 100 per cent recycled.
2 Reduce electricity and water consumption in the offices.
3 Encourage staff to re-use paper and print on both sides
4 Buy and use recycled printer ink cartridges.
5 Encourage staff to travel to work by public transportation.
6 When executives and journalists travel, encourage them to go by train.
7 Where they travel by plane, plant trees to take up the carbon dioxide emissions that this causes.

Speaking

	Last year	This year
Percentage of recycled paper used	80 per cent	84 per cent
Cost of electricity in printing plant	$2,100,000	$1,900,000
Cost of electricity in office	$420,000	$390,000
No. of employees cycling to work	27	34
Travel: number of miles flown	600,000	500,000
Number of trees planted	6,000	5,000

Vocabulary **A** Model answers

1 We have increased the amount of recycled paper that we use.

2 We gave reduced the cost of the electricity that we use in the printing plant and in the office.

3 The number of employees cycling to work has increased.

4 We have reduced the number of miles flown by our executives.

5 We have reduced the number of trees we have had to plant.

ON THE LINE **A** a3 b1 c2

Writing Model answer

Memo

From:	_____, PR officer
To:	Katherine Green
Date:	23 April 200-
Subject:	Environmental policies

As requested, this is to let you know about the enquiries I have had this year about our company's environmental policies. People mainly want to know about 1) how we encourage staff to cycle to work (45 per cent of enquiries) and 2) staff air travel, particularly our policy on tree-planting to repair the damage caused by carbon dioxide emissions (40 per cent of enquiries).

In reply, I give them the latest figures. In addition, on issue 1, I tell them about the money we give employees so that they can buy a bike, the secure bike racks that we offer and so on. On issue 2, I tell them about the organizations with which we work to plant trees all over the world. ....

Grammar review and development 21–24

present continuous for trends

A 1 The economy is growing at 7 per cent per year.

2 Construction companies are building a lot of new offices and apartments.

3 A lot of people are leaving the country and moving to cities.

4 People are earning more and more money.

5 Investors are putting a lot of money into China.

6 Foreign companies are opening new shops.

B 1 Is the population growing or falling? – It's falling.

2 Is the average increasing or decreasing? – It's increasing.

3 Is unemployment rising or falling? – It's rising.

4 Is the number of new companies going up or down? – It's going down.

5 Are people getting richer or poorer? – They're getting poorer.

6 Are people feeling more confident or less confident? – They're feeling less confident.

C 1 Twenty-five countries belong to the EU.

2 The new members include Poland, the Czech Republic and eight other countries. ✔

3 The Scandinavian members consist of Denmark, Sweden and Finland.

4 Economic growth in different countries seems to depend on a combination of factors. ✔

5 Ireland owes its success largely to its membership of the EU. ✔

6 Countries prefer to use English in discussions, rather than French.

7 Some people in the UK want to leave the EU.

present perfect with *already* and *yet*

A **1** Have you prepared the site? – We've already prepared the site but we haven't started building yet.

2 Have you built the walls? – We've already built the walls but we haven't put on the roof yet.

3 Have you connected the electricity? – We've already connected the electricity but we haven't installed the machines yet.

4 Have you installed the machines? – We've already installed the machines but we haven't started manufacturing yet.

5 Have you started manufacturing? – We've already started manufacturing but we haven't launched the product yet.

6 Have you launched the product? – We've already launched the product but we haven't sold any yet.

B **1** I've already seen him.   **4** I've already phoned them.

2 I've already written it.   **5** I've already got them.

3 I've already sent it.   **6** I've already had it.

Verb patterns

A Model answer

1 She advised me to go and see Bob about the product launch.

2 She told me to write a letter to Temco.

3 She wanted me to send a fax to GLX.

4 She told me to phone Williamson's.

5 She wanted me to get the latest sales figures from the sales department.

6 She told me to go and have lunch.

B **1** She asked me not to talk to anyone else.

2 She told me not to post it.

3 She told me not to phone them.

4 She advised me not to waste time.

5 She asked me not to give the figures to other departments.

25 A delayed project

Memo   **B** Model answer

> The installation of the electricity and computer network only happened in July and August, because of technical problems. Then the painting was only finished at the end of September because of a strike by the painters' union. We hoped to install the furniture in August, but the wrong furniture was ordered. We sent it back and got the correct furniture, but it took until the end of November to complete this phase.

E-mail exchange   **C** Model answer

> Hi Tom,
>
> I'm sorry to hear about the delayed move. I can understand why you're feeling so stressed. You could try to get some help to reduce your stress levels.
> Why not go to see a stress counsellor that I know—she's very good. The name of the counsellor is Sarah Connell and her e-mail address is s.connell@libserve.com
>
> Please find attached an article about her from Business Month magazine.
>
> I hope you like it.
>
> Good luck!
>
> All the best,
>
> Ray

D Model answer

Ray hi,

Sorry not to get back to you earlier. I contacted Sarah Connell and I had my first session with her on Friday. She's very good! I'm already feeling better.

Unfortunately, I couldn't open the attachment with the article about Sarah Connell that you sent me. Would it be possible to send it again? Many thanks.

I'll be in touch again soon.

All the best,

Tom

26 Consumer complaints

Letter **B** c a d e f b

C Model answer

Dear Sir or Madam,
I am writing about a toaster that I bought from you last month (Supertoast 100A).
The toaster is unusable because the toast always burns after just a few minutes.
I have read the instruction manual carefully and I am sure that I am following the
manufacturer's instructions correctly. The problem must be that the toaster is
defective, so I am writing to ask for a complete refund, plus an extra amount for
the inconvenience that I have experienced.
Looking forward to hearing from you,
Yours sincerely,
[your name]

Reply **A** 1e 2c 3a 4b 5d

Memo **B** Model answer

From: James Stevens, Customer Experience Manager
To: All reception staff
Date: 29 June 200-

Gizmo Electronics

Re: Customer calls

Over the past two months I have received a lot of calls from customers complaining about the attitude our staff in the call centre. Please could you put calls like these through to our call centre manager, Steve Wilkins. I have spoken to Steve about this, and he has agreed to deal with these calls.

Many thanks.

27 A new opening

Invitations **B** 1 find – found

2 news – new

3 confident – confidential

4 of – as

5 decide – decision

6 employs – employees

7 open – opening

8 attach – attached

9 you – yourself

10 allow – let

C 1 ✓ 2 to 3 of 4 ✓ 5 at 6 ✓ 7 the

E Model answer

Thank you for the invitation to your event on 15th April. This is to confirm that I would like to attend. Would it be possible to bring a colleague? Her name is Barbro Holmgren. Please could you let me have directions on how to get to the event? And please could you tell me at what time it ends?

Many thanks.

F Model answer

Thank you for your invitation to your open evening on 15th April. Unfortunately, this is a very busy time in our organisation and no one will be able to attend. I'd be grateful if you could keep us informed about similar events in the future.

Many thanks.

28 Finding an agent

Fax exchange   **B Model answer**

Dear Ms Rios,

Many thanks for your fax.

We are one of the biggest importers of food into Japan.

Your energy drink sounds very interesting.

I would very much like to meet you when come to Japan next month.

How about coming to my office on Tuesday 11th at 3 pm?

I look forward to discussing the possibilities with you.

Please could you confirm that this date is suitable?

Best regards,

Masahiko Kato

C
1	come – coming	5	paying – paid
2	discuss – discussion	6	on – about
3	last – next	7	sell – sales
4	prize – price	8	agree – agreement

D 1 b 2 c 3 d 4 a 5 d 6 b 7 b 8 c 9 a

29 Remote working

Memo   **A**
1	central	6	smaller
2	expensive	7	continue
3	doubled	8	looking
4	important	9	equipment
5	decided		

E-mail exchange

A Model answer

I often need to meet clients at our office in central London.

I need to talk colleagues about projects that we are working on together.

I often need to use the systems and equipment at the head office.

There is no space at home for computer equipment.

I really want to keep home and work separate.

I hope you understand my point of view.

B Model answer

I don't often need to meet clients in my type of work.

I work faster without interruptions from colleagues.

I already have a computer at home.

I would like these new arrangements because I will be able to spend more time with my family.

I can come to the office one day a week.

I hope you will allow me to work from home.

C
1 working	4 spoken	7 will (or can) provide
2 to see	5 see	8 have decided
3 have looked	6 need	9 will supply

D Model answer

Many thanks for your reply to my memo. Thank you for agreeing to work from home. You will start working from home on August 1st.

As you already have a computer, you will receive a special payment of £1000. If you prefer not to use your own computer, you can get a notebook computer from us.

Please could you discuss arrangements for homeworking with Caroline, your manager?

Thanks again for agreeing to this change.

30 A world trip

Text message

B 1 I've been accepted for university in September next year.

2 Me too! We must do a round the world trip in our gap year! We're Australian, after all!

3 Are you free for a drink tomorrow evening to talk about it?

4 Where do you suggest?

5 How about Gino's at 8?

6 See you there.

7 I'll bring all the guide books.

8 OK. See you then!

C Model answer

E-mail **Ⓐ** 1c 2g 3f 4h 5b 6e 7d 8a

Ⓑ 1 :-)   2 :-D   3 : @   4 :-( )   5 :-~)   6 :-X   7 :-(

Postcard **Ⓑ** Model answers

> Hi, Tom. We're having a great time in Turkey! It's very hot, but I love travelling round this beautiful country. There are so many interesting things to see. And the food is delicious! I'm not looking forward to going back to work– I want to stay here for another six months!
>
> Wish you were here,

Review and development 25–30

Ⓐ Model answers

> The painting in the reception area is still not finished.
> The lighting in the offices is too bright and needs to be adjusted.
> The carpet on the 1st floor is not stuck down and is dangerous.
> The doors to some of the offices do not fit and it is impossible to close them.
> The central heating is too hot and it's impossible to turn it down.
> As you can imagine, the senior managers are very annoyed.
> How soon can the above points be sorted out?

Ⓑ Model answers

> I have seen Sarah Connell (the stress counsellor that you recommended) about 10 times now. There was some improvement at first, but recently I have had the stress of the late move to our new offices. As you can imagine, the senior managers were extremely angry. They blamed me for not dealing with the builders efficiently. I'm now thinking about moving to another company–do you know of any job possibilities in your company?

Ⓒ
1 enjoyed   4 intend   7 chosen
2 opening   5 delighted   8 convenient
3 decision   6 consideration 9 discuss

Ⓓ Model answers

> Amajuice has been very successful in its first year in Japan. We have sold 1 million cans–twice the objective that we agreed.
>
> Our next year's objective is to sell 3 million cans.
>
> We are now interested in manufacturing Amajuice in Japan and I would like to discuss possibilities with you.
>
> We have a site available for the plant just outside Tokyo.
>
> Would it be possible for me to come to Sao Paulo in the next two weeks to discuss plans? If so, when would be suitable for you?

E
1 going
2 am coming
3 to meet
4 to book
5 has
6 am going

7 arrange
8 brought
9 is (or are)
10 helping
11 make

F **Model answer**

> Hi, Kirsti, It's been great to be in India, but now I want to go back to Australia to start university. The weather is very hot here and travelling is very tiring. I'm looking forward to a nice, comfortable room and to eating some Australian food!

G It's great to be back, but I'm nostalgic for India. Let's go to an Indian restaurant this evening. How about eight o'clock? Have you tried Khan's? It's very good. I'll bring all the pictures! See you!

Student B material

1 A working day

ON THE LINE **A**

Student B

You answer the phone at Trendex.
Trendex. Can I help you?

Student A wants to speak to Maya Nolan. He/she calls four times, but each time Maya is not available.

For each call, say where Maya is:

1 out to lunch. *She's out to lunch.*

2 out of the office seeing a client.

3 at the warehouse looking at new products

4 on holiday.

3 We're behind schedule

ON THE LINE **B**

Student B

You are Daljit. Student B is Keith. Look at the information below. Answer Keith's questions about actual spending on the Crazy Raiders project.

In the end we actually spent $450,000.

Budget (US$)	Planned	Actual
Design game	300,000	450,000
Write software	750,000	1,500,000
Design packaging	7,000	10,000
Manufacture product	92,000	133,000
TOTAL	1,149,000	2,093,000

4 Are you a team player?

ON THE LINE **C**

Student B

You are Zak, a colleague of Amanda (Student A). Today is Tuesday. Tom West was coming for a job interview on Thursday at 2 pm. But yesterday you phoned him to ask him to come on Wednesday (tomorrow) at 10 am. He agreed to come at the new time. Phone Amanda to tell her about the new interview time.

Hello Amanda. This is Zak. It's just to let you know that Tom West is coming for an interview tomorrow at 10 am, not on Thursday.

Tell her about the different times you tried to contact her.

- You left a message on her desk on Monday afternoon.

- You sent her an e-mail on Monday evening.

- You left a voicemail this morning on her answering machine at work.

- When Amanda asks you to arrange another time for the interview, you can either agree to do this or refuse. Then end the conversation.

7 Family entertainment

 B

Student B

You are the director of Farwest, Mary-Jane Lomax. Student A is a colleague who works in the PR department at Farwest. He interviewed the three visitors from France, the UK and India (Reading and listening, exercise B).

• Ask your colleague to give you the main points from each of the three interviews, and note them down. *What did the three visitors like most?*

• When your colleague asks for it, give him the average scores of the different attractions. *Visitors give the rodeo an average score of 8.92 out of 10. ...*

	Average score /10	Typical comments
Rodeo	8.92	Exciting, looks dangerous but cowboys are very professional
Country music and singing	9.13	Beautiful music, very high standards of playing
Cowboys cooking	3.36	Boring, no variety in the food. All they do is cook beans.
Roller coaster	8.42	Terrifying but good. 'Extreme' experience.
Restaurants	4.27	Not enough choice. No wine. Unattractive decor. Overseas visitors dislike service charge of 15 %.
Ranch Hotel	9.55	Comfortable, quiet, clean. Typical 'western' décor. Visitors love the big American breakfasts.
Overall satisfaction score	7.28	

• When your colleague asks for it, give him the overall score. *The overall score is ...*

• When your colleague asks for it, give him typical comments for the different attractions. *People think the rodeo is exciting. It looks ...*

Roleplay **B**

Student B

Farwest, Utah. You want to replace cowboys cooking with a shooting range. In a new building, visitors will use copies of nineteenth-century guns to shoot at targets. Total cost: $2,000,000. If you can do this, you predict the visitor satisfaction score will rise to at least 9.0, and you will have three times as many visitors: 1,500,000 per year.

Student C

Shark Paradise, Miami. You need more aggressive sharks – the ones you have are not aggressive enough. When the theme park workers throw red meat in the pool, the sharks swim the other way. Visitors are getting annoyed. You want to buy 100 new sharks at $25,000 each. Total cost: $2,500,000. If you can do this, you predict the visitor satisfaction score will rise to at least 9.5. You think you will get 3,250,000 visitors per year if you can make this investment.

Student D

Mountain Village, Japan. Visitors complain there isn't enough to do. You want to build a chair lift to the top of the mountain behind the village (2000 metres high) for use in summer (for the ride and the views) and in winter (for skiing). Total cost: $4,000,000. If you can do this, you predict the visitor satisfaction score will rise to at least 9.3. The number of visitors will rise to 2,250,000 per year.

Student E

Future City, France. Your city of the future is 20 years old and it's beginning to look out of date. You want to build a new modern cinema with all the latest special effects, including seats that shake when there is a lot of action in the film. Total cost: $4,500,000. If you can do this, you predict the visitor satisfaction score will rise to at least 8.75, and the number of visitors per year will rise to 1,500,000.

Student F

Kings and Queens, UK. Your roller coaster is not 'extreme' enough. You need to build another, more exciting one. Total cost: $3,000,000. If you can do this, you predict the visitor satisfaction score will rise to at least 9.0, and the number of visitors per year will rise to 2,250,000.

9 Getting fit

Speaking **A**

Student B

You are Jennifer Powell. Student A is a colleague. You have now visited the three health clubs in On the line. Use the information below to answer your colleague's questions about the three clubs.

	Dynamo	Elan	Fun
Convenience	Very convenient (next door to the bank).	Inconvenient – 15 minutes from the bank by subway.	Not bad – 5 minutes walk from the bank.
Changing rooms	Spotless.	Very clean.	OK.
Gym	Modern equipment.	More modern equipment than at Dynamo.	Basic. Equipment getting old.
Other facilities	Cafe open 7am–10pm – great fruit juices.	Cafe open 8am–9pm – very good sandwiches.	None.
	Small supermarket open 8am–8pm Doctor available 2–4pm. Trained in the US.	Doctor available 3 – 6pm. Expert in western and Chinese medicine	

10 Asleep on the job?

Speaking **A** *Student B*

Ask Student A questions to complete the information below.
How many hours a week do people work?

Hours	30 or less: 15%		
Shift work			—
People feel at their best			
People feel at their worst			

Then, when Student A asks for it, give them the information below.

Time for lunch	45 mins or less: 34%	45–75 mins: 57%	75 mins or more: 8%	—
Type of lunch	sandwiches: 18%	cafe or restaurant: 45%	health club cafe: 5%	company restaurant: 32%
Wine or beer with lunch	Yes: 12%	No: 88%	—	—
Tea and coffee	None: 4%	1–3 cups: 55%	4–6 cups: 34%	7 cups or more: 7%

 ON THE LINE 11 Dealing with stress

B *Student B*

It is one month later. You are Tommy Chan. Phone someone (Student A) in the human resources department at your workplace. Use the information below to have three conversations. (You are off work quite often!)

In each conversation, say you can't come into work today, and give a reason.

Hello. My name's Tommy Chan. I'm sorry I can't come into work today. I …

When Student A asks, say how long you will be off work, and answer any other questions that they have.

- Flu – you got very wet in the rain two days ago. You can't come to work again this week. You will be back on Monday.

- Food poisoning at the restaurant you went to last night. You feel terrible, but will try to come to work tomorrow.

12 Work-life balance

ON THE LINE **A**

Student B

You're Lauren Charpentier. You are phoning Joanne about your job application. Listen and complete the expressions that Lauren uses in the conversation.

Oh, hello. I hope you don't mind if I phone like this. My name's Lauren Charpentier.

I sent you an application for a job ...

I'm phoning to ask if you've had time to ...

Really. ...

Can I get back to you? I have to find someone to ...

Oh good! Who should I ask for when ...?

Great. I look forward to ...

Thank you so much ...

Speaking **A**

Student B

You are Lauren Charpentier. Joanne Samms is interviewing you for the job of web designer at Lund Edwards. Give details about your education, career, etc., when Joanne asks for them. (She has lost your CV.)

I was born on ... in Montreal.

Lauren Charpentier

Date of birth:
1 May 1968, Montreal

1979-86
Fairview High School

1987-90
University of Toronto – degree in graphic design

1990-95
Mulhouse Advertising Agency, Toronto – graphic designer
Hamsun McTaggart Horowitz design consultants, New York – senior graphic designer

1997-98
Web design qualification, University of New York

1998-now
Freelance web designer, Vancouver

Interests:
learning Spanish, gym, skiing

One child
(2 years old)

Here is some more information that you can give.

- Born in Montreal - *Your father was a French speaker and your mother an English speaker.*
- High School – *You were very good at art.*
- Toronto University – *You enjoyed your time there.*
- Mulhouse Advertising – *very good as a first job. You got a lot of experience there. You met your husband there and moved to NY with him.*
- Hamsun McTaggart Horowitz – *very good job, but very stressful.*
- Web design qualification – *you wanted to move into web design*
- Freelance web designer – *You moved to Vancouver because New York was very stressful.*
- You are applying for the job at Lund Edwards because of the attractive salary and very good benefits – especially the day care centre for your daughter.
- You have had enough of the stressful life of the freelancer – finding work, working long hours, getting paid late, etc. You want a better work-life balance.

13 Low-cost airlines

Grammar **B**

Student B

Here are some more facts about easyJet. Answer Student A's questions about events 1-3.

1 The Superbrand Council recognises easyJet as 'an outstanding brand name' – 1998 – *They did this about seven years ago.*

2 Independent Television shows its first series (of five!) about easyJet. - 1999

3 London Stock Exchange lists easyJet shares for the first time. – 2000

Now ask Student A questions about events 4–6.

4 Sir Colin Chandler takes over as chairman.
How long ago did Sir Colin Chandler take over as chairman?

5 EasyJet orders 120 aircraft from Airbus.

6 The first Airbus A319 goes into service.

ON THE LINE **B**

Student B

Listen to the conversation and complete.

I have a reservation to Barcelona on 9th June at 10.30 in the morning, but I'd like to ...
QZ ...
The 9th ...
Braithwaite – ...
That's right. I'd like to change to the 16th of June if possible.
Oh...
Let's go for ...
0...
4223 ...

Repeat the conversation. You are Rebecca and Student A is Dawn.

14 Bright ideas

Vocabulary and speaking **B**

Student B

You are Clara Rios. You go to see Jane Anderson (Student A) at BAF Venture Capital to ask for finance for your energy drink. Jane will ask you about the ingredients of the drink.

- You can't give the exact ingredients — just say they come from plants and trees in the Amazon.

  I can't tell you. It's an industrial secret! Let's just say that ...

- You need start-up capital of $10 million. You can contribute $2 million from your family members (your sister is a successful businesswoman), but you need another $8 million for the manufacturing, marketing and distribution.

These are your objectives for Year 1:

- Manufacture the product in Brazil. Launch the product in the US and Latin America, first. Market it as an energy drink. Sell it in as many places as possible (supermarkets, shops, etc.)

- Aim for sales of 10 million cans in the first year. You want to sell the drink at about $1.50, with a profit of 15 cents on each can. This would give you a profit in the first year of $1.5 million.

15 Consumer electronics

N THE LINE ❸

Student B

You are Lee Peng. You call Henry Steen (Student A) to discuss his order for DVD players. Start the conversation as in exercise A.

A: *Henry Steen here.*

B: *Hello, Henry, this is Lee Peng in Shanghai.*

A: *Hello, Mr Lee. I was expecting your call. How are you?*

B: *Fine, thank you. Thanks for your e-mail. You're going ahead with your order. That's good!*

Then continue the negotiation. You can offer the following:

- 300,000 units over 2 years: $17.50. Your minimum price is $17.25. (Below this you will lose money.) *We can offer 300,000 units over two years at a unit price of $17.50.*
- 400,000 units over 3 years: $16.50. Your minimum price $15.75. (Below this you will lose money.)
- Come to an agreement.
- Answer Henry's question on payment terms: 20% on signature of contract, the rest in relation to number of units delivered – invoices every 3 months.
- End by inviting Henry to Shanghai. *You must come to Shanghai some time.*
- Then end the conversation suitably

16 Cosmetics and pharmaceuticals

Speaking ❸

Student B

AVON	
Annual sales:	$6.2 billion
Markets:	Avon sells its products in 143 countries
Distribution:	3.9 million direct sales representatives
Product lines:	Avon Color Avon Skincare Avon Bath & Body Avon Haircare Avon Wellness Avon Fragrance beComing mark.(TM)

N THE LINE ❻

Student B

You are the caller. Use the information below to ask and answer questions.

- Ask for someone in a particular department. *Can I speak to ... in ..., please?*
- Say why you are calling and who you are.
- Thank A.

17 I'm running late

ON THE LINE ❹

Student B

Take the role of each of the people who phoned in exercise A. React as shown when you see the person you phoned (Student A) and answer their questions.

Conversation 1: You are Alain. When you arrive, you see Maggie. Say you are glad to be there and that you had a terrible journey.

Maggie: *Hi Alain. I'm glad you made it.*

Alain: *I'm glad to be here. I had a terrible journey.*

- Answer Maggie's questions. (It took you half an hour to find somewhere to park. / Next time, you are going to use the metro.)

Conversation 2: You are Cathy. When you arrive, you see Mehmet. Say hello and say you are glad to be there.

- Answer Mehmet's questions. (You don't know why the ferry was late. It left Bandirma on time but during the trip they made an announcement in Turkish that you didn't understand. / You would like an orange juice.)

Conversation 3: You are Anthea. When you arrive, you see John Randall's receptionist.

- Apologise for being late. You are annoyed that Mr Randall has cancelled the appointment – it wasn't your fault that the train was late.
- Tell the receptionist that you will come back at the time she gives you.

19 New ways of working

Speaking and vocabulary

❹

Student B

Answer Student A's questions about trends in Europe.

A: *How many mobile phone users are there in Europe now?*

B: *380 million.*

- Then ask Student A for the missing information.

How many mobile phone users were there five years ago?

	5 years ago	now	in 5 years
Mobile phone users		380 million	
Homes with broadband access	10 million		150 million
Teleworkers		80 million	

ON THE LINE ❺

Student B

You are on the train from London to Paris. Phone your colleague in Paris (Student A) three times from the train. In each conversation, say where you are and what time you expect to arrive. Use the notes below to explain why you can't hear and where you are.

- Conversation 1: Weak signal / You're just leaving London on the 15.10 train – you missed the one at 14.30. You expect to arrive at 18.10.
- Conversation 2: About to go into the tunnel / You're on the English side, just going into the tunnel. Train delayed by floods on English side. You now expect to arrive at 19.05.
- Conversation 3: Low battery / You're outside Paris, but the train has broken down. You now expect to arrive at 19.55.
- End each conversation suitably.

A: *Hi ..., where are you?*

B: *Hello ... I can't hear you very well. The signal is very weak. We're just leaving London. I'm on the 15.10 – I missed the one at 14.30.*

...

A: *OK, I'll phone you later.*

B: *Right. I'll talk to you later. Bye for now.*

Unit 20 Why travel?

ON THE LINE B

Student B

You are Bernie, head of marketing at the new low-cost airline SmartJet. You are currently on a business trip to Madrid. Your boss Alex (Student A) wants to produce some cheap newspaper advertisements in French, German and Italian. Alex organises a conference call to discuss this with you and with Chris (Student C), the head of an advertising agency in Berlin. You can produce the advertisements and get them translated at a cheap translation agency. You think this will cost €1000. However, you know this is dangerous! You're not an advertising expert, and you know the translation agency could make mistakes. When Chris says that his agency could do it, agree with him. Tell Alex that it's worth paying the extra money for a professional job.

Student C

You are Chris, head of an advertising agency in Berlin. Student A is Alex, head of a new low-cost airline, SmartJet. Alex wants to produce some cheap newspaper advertisements in French, German and Italian. Alex organises a conference call to discuss this with you and with Bernie (Student B), head of marketing at SmartJet. You can produce the advertisements and get them translated by your branches in France, Germany and Italy. You think this will cost €10,000. Alex will think this is expensive, but tell him it's even more expensive to make mistakes in advertising!

22 Made in Cambodia

ON THE LINE B

Student B

You work for a clothing company. You are on a business trip to Manila in the Philippines to find a clothing contractor there. Your colleague (Student A) phones you to check your progress. Use this information to answer their questions.

- The trip is going very well.
- You have been in Manila for four days. You have seen seven possible suppliers in that time and you have found one that you want to work with – a company called Manila Garments.
- You have discussed price and quantities with them, but you haven't agreed all the conditions of the contract. You will finalise these by email after you get back.
- You are flying back home tomorrow.

Here is a reminder of the expressions you can use:

We've made a lot of progress in the negotiations so far. / We've made good progress in the discussions so far.

We haven't talked about price yet. / We haven't discussed the price yet.

I think we can reach a deal with them. / I think we can do a deal with them.

I'll tell you what happens! / I'll let you know how I get on!

23 Tourists are everywhere

ON THE LINE **C**

Student B

You return from one of Asafla Travel's holidays – Rafting on the Zambezi – and you phone the customer relations manager to complain about a problem, related to one of the following points.

- Waterfalls – the tour leader told you to carry the boat round waterfalls.
  The leader told us to carry the boat round waterfalls.
- Late night parties – the other people on the trip wanted to party into the night, but all you wanted to do was get a good night's sleep.
- The leader asked you to put up the tents and do the cooking. You thought it was the tour leader's job to do these things.
- Mobile phone communication. You are annoyed that you were not able to use your phone during the trip.
- One of the guides wanted you to buy souvenirs from his brother's shop.
- The tour leader expected you to clean the truck.
- Complain politely and ask for suitable compensation.

24 Eco-friendly business

Speaking **A**

Student B

You're the printing manager. Use this information to tell your boss, Katherine Green, about the progress made in your area.

	Last year	This year
Percentage of recycled paper used	80 per cent	84 per cent

You calculate that the maximum percentage of recycled paper you can use is 87 per cent. There are some parts of the newspaper, as the colour magazine, that require new paper.

	Last year	This year
Cost of electricity in printing plant	$2,100,000	$1,900,000

This saving is because you recently bought more energy-efficient machines that use less electricity.

Student C

You're the office manager. Use this information to tell your boss, Katherine Green, about progress in your area.

	Last year	This year
Cost of electricity in office	$420,000	$390,000

You have reduced consumption by installing automatic switches that turn off the lights when there is no one in the room.

	Last year	This year
No. of employees cycling to work	27	34

This is the number of bikes you counted in the bike park on a typical day. The weather has been better this year, and you have given $200 to every employee who wanted to buy a new bike.

Student D

You're the travel administrator. Use this information to tell your boss, Katherine Green, about progress in your area.

	Last year	This year
Travel: number of miles flown	600,000	500,000
Number of trees planted	6,000	5,000

You have succeeded in reducing the number of miles flown by persuading journalists and executives to use video-conferencing more.

N THE LINE **B**

Student B

You make three calls to the public relations officer for *Boston World*.

- Conversation 1: You want to check some figures about the number of employees cycling to work. You think the figure for this year is 50.
- Conversation 2: You read somewhere that Boston World planted 5000 trees last year. Ask the PR officer to confirm this.
- Conversation 3: You want to meet the PR officer for lunch somewhere. Suggest the Chez Jenny restaurant at 1 o'clock on Thursday.

THOMSON

Best Practice Pre-Intermediate Coursebook
Bill Mascull

Publisher: *Christopher Wenger*
Director of Product Development: *Anita Raducanu*
Director of Marketing: *Amy Mabley*
Editorial Manager: *Howard Middle (HM ELT Services)*
Intl. Marketing Manager: *Eric Bredenberg*
Developmental Editor: *Louise Elkins*
Editor: *Virginia Marconi*
Production Management: *Oxford Designers & Illustrators*

Sr. Print Buyer: *Mary Beth Hennebury*
Associate Marketing Manager: *Laura Needham*
Photo Researchers: *Billie Porter; Suzanne Williams/ PictureResearch.co.uk*
Text Designer: *Oxford Designers & Illustrators*
Cover Designer: *Sherman & Dutton*
Printer: *Canale & C S.p.A*

Printed in Italy.
1 2 3 4 5 6 09 08 07 06 05 04

For more information contact Thomson Learning, High Holborn House, 50/51 Bedford Row, London WCIR 4LR, United Kingdom or Thomson Heinle, 25 Thomson Place, Boston, Massachusetts 02210, USA. You can visit our Internet site at http://www.heinle.com

ISBN: 1-4130-0908-5

Author's acknowledgements
The author would like to thank Chris Hartley for his help and support in the initial development of *Best Practice*.

Acknowledgements
The publishers and author are grateful to the following teachers for their advice during the development of the book: George Tomaszevski (France), James Tierney, David Massey (Italy), Marina Laso Taylor, Clark Waring (Spain), Manuel Hidalgo Iglesias, Paloma Varela (Mexico), Alicia Carturegli, Marcela S. Rodríguez (Argentina), Alex Chevrolle (China), Forrest Nelson (Japan), Peter Loughran (Hong Kong).

Photo research
Pictureresearch.co.uk

Illustrations
Mark Duffin p10; all other artwork Oxford Designers & Illustrators

Photo credits
The publishers would like to thank the following sources for permission to reproduce their copyright protected photographs:
Cover Image: Image Source/Creatas
Alamy pp 4-5 (BananaStock), 8b (BananaStock), 16-17 (Alan Copson),18r (Tim Street-Porter), 20 (Frank Chmura), 22 (Sylvain Grandadam/ Robert Harding Picture Library), 24 (Colin Anderson), 32r (Jack Hollingsworth), 43 (Johannes Denysschen), 54 (Cosmo Condina), 59 (IT Stock Free), 60r (MedioImages), 62r (©RubberBall 2004), 66r (A. Pieper/plainpicture), 70t (Chris Howes/Wild Places Photography),70br (DY Riess MD), 70bc (Robert Harding World Imagery), 74 (Image Source), 78 (RubberBall), 80 (BananaStock), 86 (Goodshoot), 94b (Jagdish Agarwal), 95 (Ingram Publishing); Courtesy of **Apple** p 46; **Aviationimages.com** pp 42b, 50 (M. Wagner); **Corbis** pp 6tl (Pablo Corral Vega), 12 (David Madison/NewSport/Corbis), 18l (Yang Liu), 25 (Jim Naughten), 27 (Jose Luis Pelaez, Inc.), 34 (Walter Hodges), 37 (Jon Feingersh), 40 (Tom Wagner), 44tr (Ramin Talaie), 47 (Claro Cortes IV), 51 (Charles O'Rear), 52 (Alan Schein Photography), 60l (Jon Feingersh), 62c (Tom Stewart), 66l (David Stoecklein), 68 (Steve Raymer), 83 (Darama), 88 (Tom Stewart); **James Fletcher** p 30; **Getty Images** pp 6tr (Ryan McVay), 6bl (Bruce Ayres), 6br (Michael Cogliantry), 8t (Ryan McVay), 9b (Steve Cole), 28 (Stephen Simpson), 32l (Michael Edwards), 32c (Chabruken), 56 (David Oliver), 62l (Mark Anderson/Rubberball), 64 (Steve Bloom), 66c (Photodisc Collection), 70bl (Jakob Helbig), 72 (Dick Luria), 76 (Manfred Rutz), 84 (Chad Ehlers), 89 (Frans Lemmens), 93 (David Bramley), 94br (Julie Toy), 94bl (Jason Dewey); **Punchstock** pp 9t (Bananastock), 36 (DigitalVision), 58 (Thinkstock); Courtesy of **Red Bull Company Limited** p 44; **Rex Features** p 42t (Stuart Clarke/SCE); Courtesy of **Sony Corporation** p 44.